PRESENTED TO

_____

BY

_____

DATE

_____

# HAS ANYONE EVER SEEN GOD?

101 QUESTIONS AND ANSWERS ABOUT GOD,
THE WORLD, AND THE BIBLE

WRITTEN BY: *Carolyn Larsen*

ILLUSTRATED BY: *Amylee Weeks*

**TYNDALE®
MOMENTUM**

*An Imprint of
Tyndale House Publishers, Inc.*

Visit Tyndale online at www.tyndale.com.

Visit Tyndale Momentum online at www.tyndalemomentum.com.

Visit the author's website at www.carolynlarsen.com.

Visit the illustrator's website at www.amyleeweeks.com.

*Tyndale Momentum* and the Tyndale Momentum logo are registered trademarks of Tyndale House Publishers, Inc. Tyndale Momentum is an imprint of Tyndale House Publishers, Inc., Carol Stream, Illinois.

*Has Anyone Ever Seen God?: 101 Questions and Answers about God, the World, and the Bible*

Designed by Jennifer Ghionzoli

Published in association with Educational Publishing Concepts, PO Box 655, Wheaton, IL 60187.

ISBN 978-1-4964-1174-7

Printed in China

| 22 | 21 | 20 | 19 | 18 | 17 | 16 |
|----|----|----|----|----|----|----|
| 7  | 6  | 5  | 4  | 3  | 2  | 1  |

# INTRODUCTION

*Faith* is belief or confidence in something, even when the object of faith cannot be fully grasped in the physical realm. A relationship with God is based on faith in him. It's a growth process of learning to accept and appreciate his grace, mercy, and love. The "instruction manual" God has given us—the Bible—helps us understand who God is and shows us how to live for him, obey him, trust him, and love him. But even with this source of amazing help and the commitment to engage in life with God through faith, we sometimes have questions.

Questions aren't wrong. In fact, they're helpful because they express a desire to learn and understand. However, it's important to search for answers to your questions from a reliable source that is true to Scripture. *Has Anyone Ever Seen God?* answers 101 frequently asked questions that are common to those who are investigating faith in Jesus Christ.

Some questions are about God and his character, his plans, and his interactions with people. Others explore God's process of creation and the world he made. And some are about the Bible itself and what it teaches about knowing, serving, and loving God. It is our hope that this book will help answer some of your questions and pave the way to a strong faith in God.

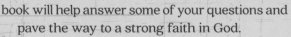

# ACKNOWLEDGMENTS

*Writing a book like this one carries with it the responsibility to be true to Scripture, to not mislead readers, and to honor and revere God. It is not something that can be accomplished alone. So I wish to thank the wonderful people at Tyndale House Publishers for their wisdom, input, and support. I appreciate Tyndale's standard of excellence and desire to honor God in every book they publish. Thank you, Anisa Baker and Becky Brandvik, for your vision for this book. Thank you to Anne Christian Buchanan for your attention to detail and "big picture" plan. It's been a privilege to work with all of you.*

*Carolyn Larsen*

# Part 1

# QUESTIONS AND ANSWERS
# ABOUT GOD

# Q. HOW DO I KNOW GOD IS REAL?

*Some people believe God is real, and they devote their lives to knowing him and living for him. But some peple say he isn't real at all. How can I know which one is right?*

A. The evidence of God's existence is all around us. Consider, for example, the fact that our planet has just the right amount of everything—oxygen, water, carbon dioxide—to support life. The earth circles our sun at just the right distance to give us warmth but not burn up in its intense heat.

Think about your complex body. It has a brain that tells your lungs to breathe, your heart to beat, your blood to flow, your arms and legs to move, and a zillion other things, and you don't even have to think about any of it. Do you think that happens by accident?

Then there is the yearning in your heart to connect with God. You long to know him, to know he loves you. That's another proof that he is real. God has put that longing in your heart because he wants to know you, too.

*Before the mountains were born, before you gave birth to the earth and the world, from beginning to end, you are God.*

PSALM 90:2

# Q. WHERE DID GOD COME FROM?

*I've been told that God made the earth and everything in it. But who made God? Where did he come from?*

**A.** Something cannot come from nothing. There would be no plants without seeds. A house can't be built without wood or a similar material. Rain and snow can't fall unless moisture condenses in the sky. Something comes from something. Nothing comes from nothing.

But the truth of this statement stops where God is concerned. God was not created by anyone or anything. God simply was . . . and is. God, Jesus, and the Holy Spirit always have been and always will be. God was already here before he made the universe and everything in it.

Is this hard to understand? Yes—because we humans are used to looking for the beginning and ending of things. Believing that God has always existed can be done only by faith. But that faith is reinforced by what the Bible—God's written Word—says about him.

He always was. He is now. He always will be.

*Your throne, O LORD, has stood from time immemorial. You yourself are from the everlasting past.* PSALM 93:2

## Q. HAS ANYONE EVER SEEN GOD?

*If not, how do we know he exists?*

A. God is a spirit, so no one knows what he looks like, and no one has ever actually seen God face-to-face. The Bible even says that if anyone did see his face, they would die because of God's great glory.

Many, many people, however, have seen God's power or felt his presence. According to the Bible, Moses saw him in a burning bush. Jesus' disciples heard him speaking from heaven. Even today, people all over the world can tell you amazing stories of how they have seen God acting in their lives.

But there is another part to this. God actually sent his Son, Jesus, to live as a human being on earth. He taught people about God. He healed the sick. He raised dead people back to life. Many people saw him, heard him, even touched him. And Jesus said that seeing him was the same as seeing God. In the life of Jesus, we get a vivid picture of just what God is like. And the Bible promises that someday we really will see him face-to-face.

*No one has ever seen God. But the unique One, who is himself God, is near to the Father's heart. He has revealed God to us.*

JOHN 1:18

## Q. IS GOD A PERSON?

*Can I touch God's hand? Can I feel his arms giving me a hug?*

A. God is a Spirit, not a person with skin. And yet God does many of the things we do. He communicates, feels emotions, and thinks. He has ideas. He acts in the world. And he connects with human beings by demonstrating his care and provision in their lives.

Can you feel God's arms around you? Yes, but not in the way you feel another person give you a hug. When you are sad or frightened or lonely and need his comfort, sit quietly and think about him; you might just feel his presence with you. You may even feel his Spirit wrapping you in a hug, reminding you that he is with you and loves you very much.

There's another important way you can feel the touch of God: through the loving words and actions of people who love him. It is a wonderfully tangible manifestation of God's personal care in our lives. Have you encountered this kind of touch?

○ ○ ○ ○ ○ ● ○ ○ ○ ○ ○ ○ ○ ○ ○ ○ ● ○ ○ ● ● ○ ○ ○ ○ ○ ○ ● ○ ○

*The Lord is the Spirit. . . . So all of us who have had that veil removed can see and reflect the glory of the Lord. And the Lord—who is the Spirit—makes us more and more like him as we are changed into his glorious image.* 2 CORINTHIANS 3:17-18

# Q. WHAT IS GOD LIKE?

*If we can't see or touch God, how do we know what he's like?*

A. Here are just a few descriptions of the God you'll get to know as you read the Bible and spend time with him in prayer:

- *God is righteous.* He is so good that sin and evil cannot coexist with him—which is why our sin is such a problem.
- *God is incredibly powerful.* He can do anything he wants—except contradict his own character.
- *God is infinitely creative.* He dreamed up our amazing world and continues to find new ways of solving the problems we create.
- *God is deeply mysterious.* If we could understand him completely, he wouldn't be God!
- *God is patient.* He doesn't see time the way we do, and he's willing to wait for everything to be made right in his world.
- *God is full of grace and mercy.* He loves us even when we don't deserve love. And if we are truly sorry when we've done wrong, he forgives us for even the most terrible things.
- *God is love.* This is the very essence of God's character—almost a definition. We can always trust God to love us and act lovingly toward us.

---

*God is love, and all who live in love live in God, and God lives in them.*   1 JOHN 4:16

**6**

# Q. ARE JESUS AND GOD THE SAME PERSON?

*They have different names, and both have several other names too. But are they actually the same person?*

A. The answer to this question is yes . . . and no. And yes, that's a bit confusing. More accurately, it's a mystery—one of those truths about God that takes a lifetime or more to understand completely.

Jesus is God's Son. God is his Father. One time Jesus said that he and his Father are one. That doesn't mean they are the same, but that they are united. Jesus also said that anyone who sees him has also seen the Father. So it's obvious that they are very, very close.

God the Father, Jesus the Son, and the Holy Spirit are all God but are also separate "persons" or manifestations that exist together in intimate relationship. The term for this threefold nature of God is the Trinity. To help explain the Trinity, the example of an egg is sometimes used. An egg has three separate parts—the shell, the white, and the yolk. All are separate, but together they are an egg.

So Jesus is not the same as God the Father, but he is still God and is a part of the Trinity: the three persons of God.

- - - - - - - - - - - - - - - - - - - - - - - - - -

*The Father and I are one.*   JOHN 10:30

## Q. WHAT (OR WHO) IS THE HOLY SPIRIT?

*What role does he play in my Christian life?*

A. The Bible clearly states that the Holy Spirit is . . . God. He is one person of the three persons who are all God and together are often called the Trinity. He has the same characteristics as God—he is everywhere, he knows our thoughts, he sees what's in our hearts, and he loves us.

The Holy Spirit has been present from the beginning of time but has a special role to play in the lives of Christian believers. Before Jesus went back to heaven after his resurrection, he said he would send the Spirit to give his followers comfort and guidance. The Spirit helps us understand the Bible. He exposes our sin and nudges us gently to return to the Father. He cares so much for us that he even prays for us when we are so upset or emotional that we can't find the words to form our own prayers. He is our Comforter, and his love for us is evident in all the ways he cares for us.

*I will send you the Advocate—the Spirit of truth. He will come to you from the Father and will testify all about me.* JOHN 15:26

# Q. IS THERE ANYTHING GOD CAN'T DO?

*God is in charge of everything, right? He is strong and powerful. Is there anything he can't do?*

A. God is indeed powerful—the Bible records a myriad of his supernatural acts. He made the world and everything in it: plants, flowers, oceans, mountains, animals, and people. The wind and weather answer to him. When he told a storm to stop, it did. At his command, the Red Sea parted and the Jordan River stopped flowing. When he told a dead man to live again, it happened. Nothing—and no one—is more powerful than God!

So is there anything God can't do? As a matter of fact, there is. God cannot be something he is not. He cannot act against his own character. He cannot tell a lie or break any of his promises. God cannot be anything less than perfect.

God cannot do those things because of who he is. It's a matter of character and identity, not ability.

*Everything is possible with God.* MARK 10:27

## Q. DOES GOD MAKE MISTAKES?

*If God is really in control of everything, why do so many bad things happen in our world? Those sure seem like mistakes. Are they?*

A. Some awful things happen in our world. That's just the truth. Tsunamis and earthquakes take lives and leave people homeless. Disease runs rampant. Children are born with birth defects or live with hunger and thirst. People do unspeakably evil things to other people.

Could God stop such bad things from happening? Of course he could.

Why doesn't he? The honest truth is, we don't know for sure. God sees things from a perspective that's different from ours, and sometimes it's hard for us to understand.

We do know that sin is at the root of the problem. When the first humans chose to disobey God, bad things started happening. It's almost as if the whole world became broken. God has been working ever since to fix it. He tells us that one day his work will be complete. In the meantime, he is with us in our pain and confusion. And he calls us to be his partners in bringing about good in the midst of the bad.

* ◦ ● ◦ ◦ ◦ ◦ ◦ ● ● ◦ ▾ ◦ ● ◦ ◦ ◦ ◦ ◦ ◦ ● ◦ ● ◦ ◦ ● ● ◦ ◦

*God's way is perfect. All the Lord's promises prove true. He is a shield for all who look to him for protection.* PSALM 18:30

# Q. IS SATAN REAL?

*Is there really a devil? Where did he come from?*

A. According to the Bible, Satan is very real, and he's nothing like the horned red creature we see in popular culture. Satan began his existence as a beautiful angel named Lucifer, created to serve God. But he rebelled, and ever since he has been at war with the good things of God—including people. Satan's whole purpose is to pull us away from God, and he does everything he can to make that happen. He is a liar and a deceiver—who disguises himself as an angel of light, which makes him especially dangerous. Sometimes, when we look at the world as it is, Satan seems to be winning.

Why hasn't God stopped Satan? He will—at the end of time. Meanwhile, God allows Satan a certain freedom in the world. But we have freedom too. We always have the choice—and the ability—to follow God and resist Satan. It's not always easy, but the Holy Spirit can help us. And when we do fall for Satan's deception, we always have the opportunity to acknowledge our mistake and come back to God.

∘ ∘ ∘ ∘ ∘ • ∘ ∘ ∘ ∘ ∘ ∘ ∘ ∘ ∘ ∘ • • ∘ ∘ ∘ ∘ ∘ ∘ ∘

*Watch out for your great enemy, the devil. He prowls around like a roaring lion, looking for someone to devour. Stand firm against him, and be strong in your faith.* 1 PETER 5:8-9

# Q. WHAT IS SIN?

*Is every wrong thing I do actually a sin?*

A. Any thought or action that falls short of what God teaches is a sin. We can sin by doing wrong things and also by *not* doing right things. But sin is not just a single choice or action. It's also an attitude and a way of being. It's disobedience, rebellion against God, and doing things our way (and Satan's way) instead of God's way.

And yes, we all do it. The Bible says clearly that every one of us sins (Romans 3:23). Sometimes we don't even know what we're doing. Sometimes we know it and can't seem to stop ourselves. And sometimes, to be honest, we don't *want* to stop. Rebellion and selfishness almost seem to be built into us.

The good news is that God has given us a way out of sin. He sent Jesus to save us from our built-in sin. He sent the Holy Spirit to help us know when we are sinning and to give us the strength to change. And when we mess up, he offers us the chance to confess our sins and be forgiven.

*Remember, it is sin to know what you ought to do and then not do it.* JAMES 4:17

## 12

## Q. IS ONE RELIGION AS GOOD AS ANY OTHER?

*There are lots of religions in the world besides Christianity. Does it really matter which one I believe, as long as I believe something?*

A. The Bible makes it clear that what—and whom—you believe in makes a big difference.

Yes, there are other forms of religion that worship or promote other beliefs, leaders, and even "gods." But none can claim the power, creativity, or strength of the true God. His power has raised dead people back to life. He offers forgiveness, love, and a personal relationship with him as our heavenly Father. Only Christianity gets to the root of humanity's deepest need—pardon from sin and escape from eternal punishment—without having to work for it or strive to earn God's favor.

It may be tempting to follow other faiths, but they cannot offer this kind of true salvation. It's comforting to know that the one true God eagerly invites us to enter into the freedom and joy that only he can give—both now and forever.

*You must not have any other god but me.*  EXODUS 20:3

## Q. DOES GOD KNOW EVERYTHING THAT WILL HAPPEN IN THE FUTURE?

*If God doesn't force us to do things—if he lets us make our own choices—then how can he know everything that is going to happen?*

A. God gives people the freedom to make choices. He has always given that freedom, which is why sin is in the world. Adam and Eve chose it. So if people can make their own choices, how can God know what will happen in the future?

The best way to understand this is to consider that even though God lets you make your own choices, he knows what choices you will make. He has a plan for what your life can be and will use your choices to guide you to the best place.

Nothing surprises God. He does know the future . . . just because he is God. And he cares about *your* future . . . because he loves you.

* * *

*I am God, and there is none like me. Only I can tell you the future before it even happens. Everything I plan will come to pass, for I do whatever I wish.* ISAIAH 46:9-10

## Q. DOES GOD SEE EVERYTHING I DO?

*Is what I do when I'm alone a secret, or does God see everything?*

A. One of God's characteristics is that he is omnipresent. That means he is everywhere, all the time. So no matter where you are, if you are in a big crowd of people or all by yourself, God sees you. He sees each thing you do. He knows when you are sleeping, watching TV, and working in the yard. There are no secrets kept from God.

You can try to keep secrets. For example, you can do something you know is wrong and never actually tell God—never confess it to him. But he knows.

That shouldn't make you feel like God spies on you. That's not how he feels about it. He sees you all the time so he can take care of you. He sees you because he loves you and wants to be with you.

○ ○ ○ ○ ○ ● ○ ○ ○ ○ ○ ● ○ ○ ○ ○ ● ○ ● ● ○ ○ ● ○ ○ ○ ○ ● ○ ○

*You see me when I travel and when I rest at home. You know everything I do.* PSALM 139:3

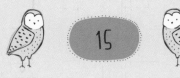

## Q. CAN GOD READ MY MIND?

*If God truly knows everything, does that mean he always knows what I'm thinking? If I have wrong thoughts, is that sin? Will I be in trouble for those?*

A. Thoughts and ideas are constantly popping into our minds. Sometimes a thought sticks around, and you think about it for a while. Sometimes it's there and gone before you know it. So does God know about all your thoughts? The answer is yes—God knows what you're thinking all the time. After all, he made your mind in the first place.

What if you have a thought that doesn't honor God—a bad thought about someone or a temptation to take advantage of another person—is that a sin? The answer to that is maybe. We can't help the thoughts that pop into our heads, but we can choose whether we let those thoughts linger. It's the lingering thoughts that can become sin if we actually act on them.

God is pleased when you push inappropriate thoughts out quickly. Those quick "get-out-of-my-mind thoughts" do not become sin. God knows about them, and he's probably proud that you pushed them out of your mind.

- - - - - - - - - - - - - - - - - - - - - - - - - - - - - -

*You know when I sit down or stand up. You know my thoughts even when I'm far away.* PSALM 139:2

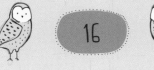

# Q. DOES GOD GET MAD AT ME?

*I've heard that God gets angry and punishes people who mess up—and I mess up all the time. What kinds of things make God angry?*

**A.** A few Bible verses tell us that God does get angry—but not over every little thing. Yes, he wants our obedience, but he doesn't get furious and "smite" us whenever we disobey. What makes God angry is when people persist in disobeying him and don't even care what he thinks—especially when those people hurt or oppress others. And even with these people, it takes God a while to get angry. He gives them many warnings, many chances to get it right before he finally gets fed up and acts in righteous anger. And even when he punishes wrongdoers, he still gives them a chance to change their ways and come back to him.

Don't worry about making God angry when you disobey him. Trust in his love and mercy. Tell him you're sorry and ask his forgiveness. He won't be angry. He will forgive you.

*The LORD is compassionate and merciful, slow to get angry and filled with unfailing love.* PSALM 103:8

# Q. WHAT MAKES GOD HAPPY?

*Does God have feelings like people do? Is he always happy? If not, then what makes him happy?*

A. The Bible begins by telling us how God created this world and then continues with stories of the things he did for his people. Another important aspect of the Bible is that it gives us instructions on how to live for God—how to make God happy. It teaches us to serve him in obedience and to love others, treating them with kindness.

As we learn to obey God more and more, he is pleased. As we learn to love and serve others—even others who aren't kind to us or those who don't care at all about God—he is pleased. In fact, God is so happy when this happens that he sings songs about delighting in us!

*The LORD your God is living among you. He is a mighty savior. He will take delight in you with gladness. With his love, he will calm all your fears. He will rejoice over you with joyful songs.*

ZEPHANIAH 3:17

# Q. WHAT DOES GOD EXPECT FROM ME?

*Does he really want me to do certain things for him?*

A. Yes, God does expect certain things of us. Meeting these expectations pleases him and makes us better people.

What does God want? First, he wants our respect. That means we recognize his power and care about what he thinks. Even more than that, God wants our love and obedience. When we love him, we will naturally respect and honor him. And when we love and respect God, we'll also show love and respect to everything God has made—especially other people. That really pleases God. In fact, Jesus said that the most important commands God gave us are to love him with every fiber of our being and to love others as much as we love ourselves.

None of this can be done in a halfhearted way. Don't expect to please God by obeying him only when you feel like it, or by saying you love him without showing love to others. Following him is a full-time job, but he is eager to help you because he has good things in store.

*What does the LORD your God require of you? He requires only that you fear the LORD your God, and live in a way that pleases him, and love him and serve him with all your heart and soul.*

DEUTERONOMY 10:12

## Q. WHAT DOES IT MEAN TO FEAR GOD?

*Does God really want us to be afraid of him?*

**A.** This answer must be divided into two parts. People who haven't accepted Jesus as their Savior should fear the judgment they will face someday for their sins. That judgment is being excluded from spending eternity with God in the Kingdom of Heaven.

But there's another definition for *fear*. It doesn't only mean to be afraid. It can also mean having a reverent awe for something or somebody. And that's the kind of fear that applies to people who follow God. We certainly don't need to be afraid to talk with God or to come to him with problems, but we should approach him with deep respect and awe because he is great and powerful, amazing and mysterious. We should treat him like he is God and take him seriously.

*Serve only the LORD your God and fear him alone. Obey his commands, listen to his voice, and cling to him.*

DEUTERONOMY 13:4

# Q. CAN I TRUST GOD?

*Does God really love me? Can I trust him to always take care of me?*

A. It's impossible to trust someone, including God, if you don't believe that person really loves you. For some of us, that kind of trust is difficult. Is it hard for you to believe God loves you since you can't see him in person or because he doesn't seem to answer your prayers? Is it hard to trust him because important people in your life have been untrustworthy?

It's okay if you have doubts about this. God understands your fears and hesitations. But men and women throughout the ages have found that trusting in God is worth the risk. God loves you and will never leave you. When he doesn't do what you ask, it's because he sees the bigger picture and knows what is best for you. You can trust him to guide you and help you make good choices. You can trust him to protect you from Satan and his evil ways. When you let yourself believe that God does all those things for you, you'll know he can be trusted . . . completely.

° ° ° ° ° • ° ° ° ° ° ° ° ° ° ° ° ° ° • ° • ° ° ° ° ° ° ° ° ° °

*The Lord directs the steps of the godly. He delights in every detail of their lives. Though they stumble, they will never fall, for the Lord holds them by the hand.* PSALM 37:23-24

# Q. WHY DOES GOD LET BAD PEOPLE SUCCEED?

*Some people don't care about God. They don't try to obey him at all. Why does God let good things happen to them?*

A. Sometimes it does seem that good things happen for people who don't care about God at all. They are often famous and successful, and many have beautiful families. It seems as if everything they touch turns to gold. Why does that happen? Why would God bless people so wonderfully when they don't honor him?

What you need to understand is that God sees a bigger picture. The good things that happen in this life really do not mean much in the big picture of eternity. Some people may have tremendous success during this life, but if they do not honor God and follow Jesus, their eternity will be spent without him. In spite of their earthly success, they will have forsaken the truest of all riches—and they will be sorry.

*LORD, you always give me justice when I bring a case before you. So let me bring you this complaint: Why are the wicked so prosperous? Why are evil people so happy? You have planted them, and they have taken root and prospered. Your name is on their lips, but you are far from their hearts.* JEREMIAH 12:1-2

# Q. WHY DOES GOD ALLOW SIN?

*Wouldn't things just be easier if God stopped all sin? Why doesn't he do that?*

A. Sometimes it seems it would be easier if God just reached out and physically stopped us before we could do anything wrong. But it doesn't really happen that way. God has the power to force people not to sin, but he doesn't do that.

Why? It's because he created us with free will. He wants us to choose to love and obey him. But we can also choose to turn away from God instead of turning to him.

Here's another possible reason God doesn't stop people from sinning. Each time we sin and come to him to ask forgiveness, we learn more about what sin is and why it's a problem. We also have the opportunity to learn more about God and experience his gracious forgiveness.

Sin is never a good thing. But God is always good—good enough to give us full freedom and good enough to handle it when we make wrong choices.

*All glory to God, who is able to keep you from falling away and will bring you with great joy into his glorious presence without a single fault.* JUDE 1:24

## Q. DOES GOD EVER CHANGE HIS MIND?

*Do my prayers have an influence on what God is going to do?*

A. There are stories in the Bible where it seems that God did change his mind in response to the requests of his people. But Christians disagree as to whether that's what actually happened.

Some say that God never changes his mind—that in those Bible stories, God knew what would be prayed and had already decided how to answer the prayer.

Others say that our prayers can certainly change God's mind as he listens to what is on our hearts. When he sees how strongly we feel, he does change his mind.

Whatever you believe, you can be sure that God knows everything and that his plans are the very best for you and for those you love. He wants you to pray because he wants to know what is important to you. You can always trust God to do what is best.

⚬ ⚬ ● ⚬ ⚬ ⚬ ⚬ ⚬ ⚬ ● ⚬ ● ⚬ ⚬ ⚬ ⚬ ⚬ ⚬ ⚬ ⚬ ⚬ ⚬ ⚬ ● ⚬ ⚬ ⚬ ⚬ ⚬

*Whatever is good and perfect is a gift coming down to us from God our Father, who created all the lights in the heavens. He never changes or casts a shifting shadow.* JAMES 1:17

# Q. DOES GOD HAVE A SENSE OF HUMOR?

*Does God actually laugh? What kinds of things does he think are funny?*

A. You can be very sure that God has a sense of humor. The best evidence of that is . . . you! The Bible tells us that people are made in the image of God. That means God created each one of us to uniquely reflect aspects of who he is. Pretty amazing, isn't it?

So since you like to laugh and you have a good sense of humor, it's safe to say that God does also. Another way to see God's sense of humor is to look around. Notice some of the things he created: giraffes with really long necks, squid with all those tentacles swooshing through the water, and giant flowers that take decades to bloom and smell really terrible. (Yes, they really exist!) You can imagine that God smiled or even chuckled when he came up with the ideas for some of his creations.

○ ○ ○ ○ ○ ● ○ ○ ○ ○ ○ ○ ○ ○ ○ ○ ○ ● ● ○ ○ ○ ○ ○ ● ○ ○

*God created human beings in his own image. In the image of God he created them; male and female he created them.*

GENESIS 1:27

# Q. IS IT WRONG TO QUESTION GOD?

*Is it okay if I ask God questions when I don't understand certain things?*

A. You will read many questions in the Bible. The writers of the Bible wondered where he was when they couldn't feel his presence. They asked why he did things in certain ways. They asked for his guidance. Sometimes his answers to their questions are given in the Bible too.

It is fine if you ask God questions. He is strong enough to handle your questions and even your honest doubts. He gave you a mind to think with, and he wants you to use it. Just be careful to be respectful of God when you ask questions. Give him the honor he deserves. Remember that he loves you and wants you to learn and grow stronger in your faith.

---

*If you need wisdom, ask our generous God, and he will give it to you. He will not rebuke you for asking.* JAMES 1:5

# Q. DOES GOD LOVE EVERYONE OR JUST CHRISTIANS?

*Does God only love people who love him back? Does he love people who are his enemies?*

A. We humans tend to love people who are like us, people we are comfortable being around. We usually find it hard to love those who are unkind to us or have committed serious wrongs. We don't need to agree with their sinful choices, but we should love even those people if we follow God's example. God loves everyone, even people who do not care about him. His greatest wish is that everyone would love him back and love one another.

God showed his love by sending Jesus to earth. It was a big sacrifice for Jesus to leave heaven and come to teach people about God, to suffer and die for the sins of all people. That's good proof of God's love for everyone.

— — — — — — — — — — — — — — — — — — — — — — —

*This is how God loved the world: He gave his one and only Son, so that everyone who believes in him will not perish but have eternal life.* JOHN 3:16

# Q. DOES GOD CONTROL EVERYTHING?

*Does God decide everything that happens in the world? Is he the boss of everything?*

A. God made everything there is. He put the sun and moon in the sky. He hung the stars. God also controls all of nature. He makes the oceans stay in place and decides where rivers will flow. He makes trees grow strong and causes even the tiniest flower to push up between the rocks. He controls when the sun rises and sets. One time, God even answered a prayer to make the sun stand still!

God doesn't just control nature. Basically, he can control anything he wants to. But here's the interesting twist: God is in control . . . and yet he chooses not to control our choices. He gives humans free will and the power to choose whether to listen to him and obey him. Because of this freedom, sometimes it feels like God isn't really in control. But never fear. In the big picture, God has his way with everything, and everyone will eventually answer to him.

*The LORD . . . has sworn this oath: "It will all happen as I have planned. It will be as I have decided."* ISAIAH 14:24

# Q. WHY DID GOD SEND JESUS INTO THE WORLD?

*If Jesus is God's only Son, why would he send him to earth and let him suffer so many terrible things?*

A. God created humans to live in intimate relationship with him and with one another, but their sin broke the beautiful harmony of creation. The only natural consequence for that sin was pain and death.

But instead of giving up on his beloved humans, God kept offering ways for them to return to him. He gave them laws for how to act and rituals to help them move past sin. He even disciplined them like a loving parent, letting them suffer the results of their sin so they would be motivated to change their ways. But people still kept getting it wrong. They were so caught up in their sin that there was no way out.

Finally God sent Jesus to show people how to live and to reconnect us with God. Jesus ended up dying on the cross for our sake—the ultimate sacrifice to save us from our sin. Then he rose from the dead, showing that not even death can win against God's love.

*This is real love—not that we loved God, but that he loved us and sent his Son as a sacrifice to take away our sins.* 1 JOHN 4:10

# Q. DOES BECOMING A CHRISTIAN MEAN LIFE WILL BE EASY?

*Some people think everything will be great after they accept Jesus. Is that true? Or do Christians still have problems?*

A. Becoming a Christian does not mean we will never have another problem. In some cases, it might mean we have *more* problems. All of us live in a world where many do not honor God and where sin prevails. Life isn't easy, even for those who have accepted Christ as Savior.

So what difference does being a Christian make? The difference is that God doesn't leave you alone to deal with your problems. He is with you in good times and bad. He gives you strength to deal with difficulties. He provides wisdom to figure things out. He gives a sense of peace and rest even in the midst of hard times. He is with you every step of the way. And he gives you human companions in the struggle— his church, the community of believers. God never meant for his people to go through hard times alone. He wants us to turn to each other, pray for each other, and support each other. Don't be afraid to call on your fellow Christians for help during hard times.

○ ○ ○ ○ ○ ○ ○ ○ ○ ○ ○ ● ○ ○ ○ ○ ○ ○ ○ ○ ○ ○ ○ ○ ○ ○ ○ ○

*Nothing can ever separate us from God's love . . . not even the powers of hell.* ROMANS 8:38

# Q. IS GOD ALWAYS TRUTHFUL?

*Sometimes people I trust say things that aren't true. Does God do that? Or can I trust everything his Word says?*

A. It's true that people disappoint you sometimes. They may not mean to, but it happens. Someone you trust promises something without really thinking things through, and the promise can't be kept. Or something is said unkindly that just isn't true. Some people tell a lot of lies on purpose, but even the best people are not always truthful. If you're honest, you'll have to admit that neither are you.

With that in mind, isn't it wonderful to know that God is *always* truthful? You can completely trust everything in his Word.

God is God, which means he cannot lie. He isn't like a person who changes his or her mind or tries to impress others. Whatever you read in God's Word, you can believe and trust. You can count on him to always keep his promises.

○ ○ ○ ○ ○ ● ○ ○ ○ ○ ○ ○ ○ ○ ○ ○ ○ ○ ● ● ● ○ ○ ○ ○ ○ ○ ● ○ ○

*God is not a man, so he does not lie. He is not human, so he does not change his mind. Has he ever spoken and failed to act? Has he ever promised and not carried it through?* NUMBERS 23:19

## Q. HOW DOES GOD SHOW HIS PRESENCE TODAY?

*We don't usually see outright miracles like those in the Bible, and we don't have Jesus walking around with us. How do we know that God is with us?*

A. We all want to feel God's presence, to have assurance that he is real. And he does show himself to us, but sometimes we must pay close attention to perceive him.

Start by praying and asking God to show himself to you. Then watch for his answer. It might not arrive in the form you expect. You might need to get away from your busy life and be quiet. It might help to seek out a special place or thing that reminds you of God—the ocean, a garden, a pet.

Don't forget to meet together with other Christians. Jesus promised to be there when two or three gather in his name. Praying and praising and talking with one another is a great way to feel his presence.

If you need God to reveal himself to you, you can be sure he will. When it happens, write down what it was like. Rereading your words can strengthen your faith as you continue seeking him.

*Where two or three gather together as my followers, I am there among them.*   MATTHEW 18:20

# Q. WHY DOES GOD SOMETIMES SEEM TO HIDE?

*Sometimes it seems as if God is hiding from me or is completely absent. Why does he let that happen? Is he really hiding?*

A. Even people who have been Christians for decades have times when God just doesn't seem to be there. Could he actually be hiding from us? And why would he do that?

Some say that God doesn't really pull his presence back at all—that for one reason or another, we just stop being able to perceive him for a while. Others believe there really are times when God turns his face from us. If he isn't readily available, maybe we will feel compelled to seek him out more passionately. Maybe we will learn to be more patient and wait for him.

Whatever the case may be, the truth is that God is always there, whether we feel his presence or not. If we persist in faith, sooner or later he will show himself once more. And even when we can't see him, he sees us—and watches over us in love.

*O Lord, how long will you forget me? Forever? How long will you look the other way?... But I trust in your unfailing love. I will rejoice because you have rescued me.* PSALM 13:1, 5

## Q. WHERE DOES GOD LIVE?

*Does God literally live in heaven, or is he kind of just everywhere?*

A. You would expect God to have a very grand home, wouldn't you? And he does. We know from the Bible that God's heaven is more beautiful than we can ever imagine. It's like nothing we have here on earth. It is built with gold and jewels and is a wonderful place where we can live with him someday. When Jesus went back to heaven, he said he would prepare a place there for each of us.

But God doesn't just sit in his heaven and look down on us. God is everywhere. His presence fills the whole earth. He is with every person on earth. So the best answer to this question is that God lives everywhere.

*"Can anyone hide from me in a secret place? Am I not everywhere in all the heavens and earth?" says the* LORD.

JEREMIAH 23:24

## Q. DOES GOD KEEP HIS PROMISES?

*God makes a lot of promises in the Bible. Will he really keep all of them? Every one?*

A. You can read in the Bible that God promises to love you and take care of you, to help you and hear your prayers. He promises to help you grow into a more mature Christian. He also makes promises about judgment and what is to come for those who reject Jesus' offer of forgiveness. He makes a lot of promises. Will he keep them all?

Yes, he will. God can be trusted completely. He keeps every word of every promise he has made. He is true to his Word because he loves his children. He wants to do everything for you that he says he will. God is so pure that he is not even capable of breaking his promises. He couldn't, even if he wanted to . . . but he doesn't want to.

° ° ° ° ° ° ° ° ° ° ° ° ° ° ° ° ° ° ° ° ° ° ° ° °

*God has given both his promise and his oath. These two things are unchangeable because it is impossible for God to lie. Therefore, we who have fled to him for refuge can have great confidence as we hold to the hope that lies before us.*

HEBREWS 6:18

# Q. DOES GOD REALLY HAVE TIME TO BOTHER WITH JUST ONE PERSON?

*God has a lot of really serious stuff to take care of. Does he have time to hear my prayers and care about what happens to me?*

A. God loves you so very much. There is no question that he has time for you . . . as much time as you want. He wants to hear your prayers, your hopes, your dreams. He wants to know what you struggle with. He cares about what frightens you.

Sure, God has the whole world and every person in it to take care of. But he is big enough to care for you as if you were his only priority.

The Bible says that God knew you before you were even born. He knows every detail of your whole life—even days you haven't lived yet. He puts a lot of time and energy into knowing you, simply because he loves you.

- - - - - - - - - - - - - - - - - - - - - - - - - - -

*You saw me before I was born. Every day of my life was recorded in your book. Every moment was laid out before a single day had passed.* PSALM 139:16

# Q. WHERE IS GOD WHEN TERRIBLE THINGS HAPPEN?

*Every day the news outlets seem full of terrible news. War. Terrorist attacks. Refugees. Human trafficking. Where is God in all of this?*

A. Remember that Satan does his work in the world because people choose sin rather than God. And God allows those choices because he has chosen to give us free will. Does that mean he doesn't care? No, not at all. God's heart breaks when people suffer, just as ours do. And we can be sure that he is close to those who suffer when terrible things happen. Comforting them. Loving them. Drawing them close. Those who know him do not die alone.

Someday the people who do evil in this world will answer to God for their actions. They won't get away with the terrible things they have done. Remember that God sees a bigger picture than we do, and what matters most to him is people spending eternity with him.

- - - - - - - - - - - - - - - - - - - - - - - - - -

*The faithful love of the LORD never ends! His mercies never cease. Great is his faithfulness; his mercies begin afresh each morning.* LAMENTATIONS 3:22-23

## Q. WHY DOES GOD ALLOW PEOPLE TO SUFFER?

*Why doesn't God protect his people from painful things? Doesn't he love them?*

A. First of all, God doesn't *cause* his children to suffer. Our pain is the result of living in a world tainted by sin. However, God does sometimes *allow* our suffering. He doesn't like seeing his children in pain. But he does often use that pain for a good purpose.

There are things to be learned from suffering if we have the right attitude of depending on God. God knows that humans learn the most from hard times. If life is always easy and we never have any problems, we may never seek God. We may not even realize we need him. But when the props are taken out of our lives, that's when we turn to God for help. We learn to lean on him and wait for his answers. In the process, we learn strength, patience, and confidence. Our faith tends to grow more during difficult times than it does when things are easy.

*We can rejoice, too, when we run into problems and trials, for we know that they help us develop endurance. And endurance develops strength of character, and character strengthens our confident hope of salvation.* ROMANS 5:3-4

## Q. CAN GOD FEEL OUR PAIN?

*Sometimes my body hurts. Sometimes my heart hurts. Can God really understand what I'm going through?*

A. God knows that life is hard. He knows that sometimes you are physically sick and in pain. He knows you can suffer emotionally, too—when you lose someone you love or when you are rejected by other people.

How do we know that God understands these things? In the first place, he made us, so he knows we're designed with the capacity to feel both joy and sorrow, pleasure and pain. But even more important, God understands pain because his Son, Jesus, lived on earth as a flesh-and-blood human being. Jesus knew what it was like to feel hunger, thirst, rejection, loneliness, temptation, and physical agony.

And most important, God cares about your pain and suffering. He asks you to pray to him and tell him your problems. He hears your cries for relief. And while he doesn't always take the pain away, he sticks close beside you when you are hurting. He gives you strength, help, and comfort.

*He was despised and rejected—a man of sorrows, acquainted with deepest grief.* ISAIAH 53:3

# Q. DOES GOD LISTEN WHEN PEOPLE TALK TO HIM?

*I tell God lots of things that I am concerned about. I ask him to do things too. Does he really listen?*

A. The best way for friends to have a good relationship is to make time to talk. So God *wants* his children to talk to him. He says that he wants to hear what you are scared or worried about. He wants to know your happy news. He wants to hear your praise. He promises that he will listen and answer.

You can be completely honest with God. That means you do not have to pray what you think he wants to hear. You can be more honest with God than you are with anyone else because he knows what you are thinking and feeling anyway.

God loves you. That's why he wants to communicate with you. You talk to him in prayer, and he answers by impressing truths from his Word in your mind and by putting thoughts in your heart.

○ ○ ○ ○ ○ ○ ○ ○ ○ ○ ● ● ○ ● ○ ○ ○ ○ ○ ○ ○ ○ ○ ● ○ ○ ○ ○ ● ● ○

*If my people who are called by my name will humble themselves and pray and seek my face and turn from their wicked ways, I will hear from heaven and will forgive their sins and restore their land.* 2 CHRONICLES 7:14

## Q. HOW DOES GOD SPEAK TO PEOPLE TODAY?

*Since I can't hear God speak in an audible voice, how do I know when he is speaking to me?*

A. God does not speak to every person in the same way. He knows the best way to speak to each of us so that we will hear him and understand.

Many Christians have the experience of hearing God speak through the Bible. As they spend time reading and studying, they hear his words and thoughts and get to know him. Sometimes a particular passage or phrase will seem to stand out in a way it never has before—a direct word from God.

God definitely speaks through the beauty of his creation. Many people feel closest to him at the seashore or hiking in the mountains. Others connect with God through music that touches their hearts. God also speaks through certain experiences in which we see his care and guidance—often in retrospect. And God definitely speaks through other people, especially older people who have known him a long time.

God will find a way to speak to you. You just need to be quiet and listen so you can hear him. And the more time you spend with God, the easier it will be to recognize when he is speaking.

*Be still, and know that I am God!*   PSALM 46:10

# Q. HOW DO WE SEE GOD'S POWER?

*I know the Bible says God is all powerful. What are some ways I can see his power each day?*

A. God's power is seen in many ways, but the most obvious way is probably in nature—churning oceans, erupting volcanoes, magnificent snowfalls. His power in the natural world can be both scary and majestic!

Another place we can see God's power is in people's lives. God—in his power—guides, directs, teaches, protects, and strengthens. You can see his power at work in how he cares for those who trust him.

Once in a while something happens that you know could only have happened by God's power. Maybe it's an answer to a seemingly impossible prayer request. Maybe it's a surprise so awesome it could not have happened on its own. Maybe it's finding you can accomplish something for God that you could never, ever do on your own.

The more you look for displays of God's power—both big, obvious ones and quieter, gentler ones—the more you'll see them, and the more your faith will grow. And remember that God is always working powerfully on your behalf.

*Through your faith, God is protecting you by his power until you receive this salvation, which is ready to be revealed on the last day for all to see.*   1 PETER 1:5

# Q. DOES GOD STILL PERFORM MIRACLES TODAY?

*God did some awesome miracles in the Bible, like parting the waters of the Red Sea and raising someone from the dead. Do they still happen today?*

A. Miracles are wondrous and amazing—and God definitely still does them. But there is more than one kind of miracle.

Occasionally God acts in a way that seems to suspend the laws of nature—like instantly healing a very sick person. Such miracles are relatively rare. Only God knows why he does them. And *not* seeing them doesn't mean God is not present or that he doesn't care.

Then there are the everyday miracles we sometimes don't even notice because we are so used to them. The sun rising and setting each day—that's a wondrous and amazing thing. So is a caterpillar turning into a butterfly or a baby forming in the womb. The fact that something happens every day and seems normal doesn't mean it's not miraculous.

The most amazing kind of miracle is when God works inside of us and helps us become more like Jesus. This may take some time, but it's still a miracle. And when someone accepts Christ as Savior—that kind of wondrous, amazing event makes the angels in heaven rejoice!

*You are the God of great wonders! You demonstrate your awesome power among the nations.* PSALM 77:14

## Q. DOES GOD MICROMANAGE MY LIFE?

*Does he watch me every minute and jump on me as soon as I break a rule?*

A. Being micromanaged means that every move we make and every word we speak is dictated by someone else. It's not a fun way to live.

God does have rules for people to obey—rules that will make life better for all. He teaches those rules in the Bible, and if we stay close to him, he helps us keep those rules. But God never forces us to obey. He gives every one of us the freedom to make our own choices. It's our choice to obey or not. It's our choice to know God or not. Every day we get to choose whether we will be kind or selfish, wise or foolish, loving or unloving.

God doesn't make us do anything. But the better we get to know him, the more we understand his love and the more we desire to please and obey him. He doesn't force us to do right. We *want* to do right.

° ° ° ° ° ° ° ° ° ° ° ° ° ° ° ° ° ° ° ° ° ° ° ° ° ° ° ° ° °

*You have been called to live in freedom, my brothers and sisters. But don't use your freedom to satisfy your sinful nature. Instead, use your freedom to serve one another in love.* GALATIANS 5:13

# Q. WHAT DOES GOD CARE ABOUT MOST?

*Is he most concerned with how much I pray and read the Bible? What's most important to him?*

A. God cares that you read the Bible because it contains his words to you. It's sort of a training manual for how to live in a way that respects, serves, and honors him. It also tells you how very much he loves you.

And yes, God cares that you pray because that is your opportunity to communicate with him and tell him what's on your heart. He cares about your obedience to him and that you do your best to stop sinning and to love other people as much as you love yourself.

But what does God care about most? Simply stated, he cares that you know him. That's why he sent his beloved Son to earth in the first place—to make a way for people to know him and to be cleansed from their sin so they can join him in heaven someday.

° ° ° ° ° ° ° ° ° ° ° ° ° ° ° ° ° ° ° ° ° ° ° ° ° ° °

*God our Savior . . . wants everyone to be saved and to understand the truth.*   1 TIMOTHY 2:3-4

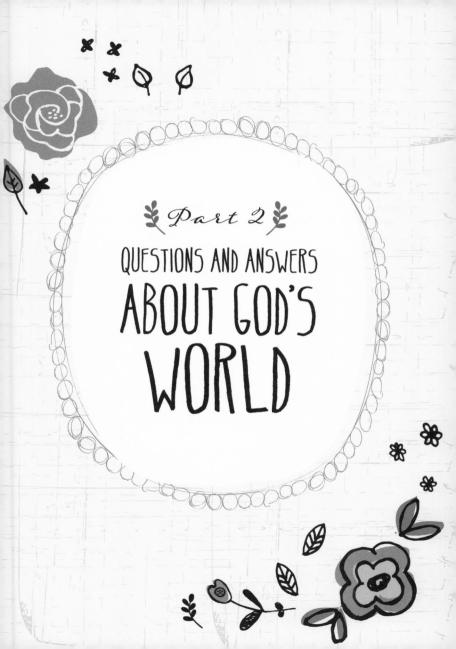

Part 2

QUESTIONS AND ANSWERS
ABOUT GOD'S
WORLD

# Q. WHAT DOES THE BIBLE TEACH ABOUT HOW THE WORLD CAME TO BE?

*I've heard that God created everything there is—but I've heard other explanations too. How do I know which one is right?*

A. The Bible teaches that God made all of creation by simply speaking it into existence. He started by creating light on the first day. Then he spent five more days making the sky, oceans, land, sun, moon, stars, plants, animals, and finally, human beings.

The very first pages of the Bible detail what God made on each day. At the end of each day, he looked at what he had made and liked what he saw. And then, when God finished making everything he wanted to make, he took an entire day to rest.

Now, no one knows whether these "days" were actual twenty-four-hour periods. The term could possibly refer to longer periods of time. There are other aspects of these early accounts that could be understood more than one way. But a few things are completely clear:

One, God created everything.

And two, everything God created was very, very good.

‒ ‒ ‒ ‒ ‒ ‒ ‒ ‒ ‒ ‒ ‒ ‒ ‒ ‒ ‒ ‒ ‒ ‒ ‒ ‒ ‒ ‒ ‒ ‒

*In the beginning God created the heavens and the earth.... And God saw that it was good.* GENESIS 1:1, 10

# Q. WHY DID GOD CREATE THE WORLD?

*If God knows everything, surely he knew what a mess humans would make of the world. So why did he create the world and put people in it?*

A. God created the world and all that is in it for his glory. Think about this beautiful world—grand mountains with beautiful waterfalls, huge oceans teeming with life, crimson sunsets and brilliant rainbows, and untold varieties of animals, from the tiniest amoeba to the gigantic blue whale. All of it reveals God's amazing power and creativity.

Human beings are God's grandest creation, the most complex and intricate. We are special because we are made to be like God and have a relationship with him. God created humans so he could enjoy us and so that we could glorify him by showing his love, mercy, and grace to others.

Did he know what a mess we humans would make of things? Well, he's God, so he knows everything. But he must have thought we were worth it because he went right ahead with his plans and has never given up on us.

---

*Holy, holy, holy is the LORD. . . . The whole earth is filled with his glory!* ISAIAH 6:3

## Q. WHY DID GOD MAKE SPIDERS, SNAKES, AND OTHER CREEPY THINGS?

*It's easy to see the good in most of God's creation. But what about creatures like snakes, mosquitoes, and spiders? Why did God make them?*

A. It's true that some creatures can make our lives kind of miserable. Others can be downright frightening. But did you ever think about the fact that most creatures have a purpose, even the ones that make our skin crawl?

Take insects, for example. Some of them eat other insects that are nuisances (think of spiders eating flies). Some provide food for animals we enjoy, such as birds. Some are invaluable for scientific research. And some, such as bees, make honey and pollinate plants. In certain countries, insects are even considered to be a source of food for humans.

So while insects may be creepy and scary, many of them clearly serve a good purpose. The same is true for other animals, such as snakes. God knew what he was doing with every single thing he made.

*The LORD made the earth by his power, and he preserves it by his wisdom. With his own understanding he stretched out the heavens.* JEREMIAH 10:12

## Q. HOW DID GOD MAKE THE FIRST MAN?

*Was Adam a full-grown man? Was he ever a baby or a child?*

A. Adam is the name of the first human being who ever lived on earth. (The same word in Hebrew is used to refer to humankind.) The Bible says that God created Adam on the sixth day of the creation week. We don't know how God went about creating water and rocks and plants and animals. But we do know that when he made Adam, he gathered up dust or clay from the ground and shaped it into a man. Then he breathed life into that man.

Adam was an adult right away. He never experienced being a baby or a small child. We know he was older than a child because God gave him jobs to do right away—like naming all of the animals. The Bible tells us Adam was made in God's image, which means he was like God. He could think and make decisions. He could be creative and care for the earth and the other creatures.

*The LORD God formed the man from the dust of the ground. He breathed the breath of life into the man's nostrils, and the man became a living person.* GENESIS 2:7

# Q. HOW DID GOD MAKE THE FIRST WOMAN?

*Was the first woman made from dust like the first man?*

A. According to the Bible, God made Adam fall into a deep sleep. While he was sleeping, God took a rib out of Adam's side and used that bone to form the first woman—created in God's image just like the man. Adam called her Eve.

Why didn't God use dust to make Eve as he did to make Adam? Perhaps God used a part of Adam to make her because he wanted Adam and Eve to be a team. They were composed of the same material. Adam put it this way: "[She] is bone from my bone and flesh from my flesh" (Genesis 2:23). God made Eve to be Adam's partner in life and to help him take care of the beautiful home God created for them—the Garden of Eden.

° ° ° ° ° ° ° ° ° • • ° ° ° ° ° ° ° ° ° • ° ° ° ° ° °

*The LORD God caused the man to fall into a deep sleep. While the man slept, the LORD God took out one of the man's ribs and closed up the opening. Then the LORD God made a woman from the rib, and he brought her to the man.* GENESIS 2:21-22

## Q. WHY DID GOD MAKE EVE?

*God had already made the first man and given him jobs to do. Why make another human?*

A. There are a couple of reasons that God made Eve. One was that he was concerned for Adam. God made all the animals to live in the Garden of Eden, and then he made Adam. But God saw that Adam was lonely. The animals couldn't share in his life the way another human would. So one reason God made Eve was for her to be a companion and friend to Adam. She could also help him take care of the Garden.

Another reason for God to make a woman was so that Adam and Eve could have children, create a family, and begin to fill the earth with people. In fact, God told them to do just that.

○ ○ ○ ○ ○ ● ○ ○ ○ ○ ○ ○ ○ ○ ● ○ ○ ● ● ○ ○ ○ ○ ○ ○ ○ ○

*Then God blessed them and said, "Be fruitful and multiply. Fill the earth and govern it."* GENESIS 1:28

# Q. HOW ARE HUMANS DIFFERENT FROM ANIMALS?

*The Bible says we are made in God's image. What does that mean? How are human beings different from animals or God's other creations?*

A. We humans are made to be more like God than anything else he made. We are more intelligent than animals. We can think and make decisions. God gave us the freedom to make our own choices. We have language and can communicate with one another in complex ways. We are creative and can show that distinction by making art and music and inventing things. We are relational—that is, we build friendships and we love our families. We have morals, which means we respect others and try to live by God's laws. We are not always successful at this, but we have a conscience and may feel guilt when we disobey God. Most important, we have spirits that can commune with God and are meant to live in eternal relationship with him.

That's not to say that animals cannot communicate, solve problems, or have relationships. Many are quite intelligent. But the Bible makes it clear that people are special. We alone are made in the image of the living God.

*God said, "Let us make human beings in our image, to be like us."*
GENESIS 1:26

## Q. WHAT WAS THE GARDEN OF EDEN?

*Where was it? What happened to it?*

A. The Garden of Eden was the home God created for Adam and Eve. It was filled with everything they needed—food, water, and incredible beauty. Animals roamed peacefully, and all kinds of plants and flowers grew there. Everything in the Garden was available for their use—except one thing. God told them not to eat from the "tree of the knowledge of good and evil" in the center of the Garden. When Adam and Eve broke that rule, God banished them from the Garden. But he still cared for the man and woman he had made and provided for them as they learned to cultivate the land and started a family. They never lived in that beautiful place again, but God also never gave up on them or their descendants.

The Bible mentions four rivers that flowed in the Garden. Two were named the Tigris and the Euphrates. There are two rivers named that today, but there is no evidence of a garden like Eden anywhere around them. Perhaps the Garden was completely wiped out in the great Flood of Noah's day. To this day no one has found it.

*The LORD God planted a garden in Eden in the east, and there he placed the man he had made.* GENESIS 2:8

# Q. WHY DID GOD GIVE HUMANS THE OPPORTUNITY TO CHOOSE EVIL?

*If God knows everything, then he knew that Adam and Eve would break his one rule about eating from that tree. So why did he even put the tree in the Garden?*

A. God created the human race to be like him and to share his love. In order for that to happen, he had to give people the freedom to make choices. He gave Adam and Eve one rule to obey. They had the freedom to choose to obey or disobey God's rule. They chose not to obey, which surely disappointed God. But it was their free choice.

We, too, have the freedom to choose to obey or not to obey God, to love God or not to love him. If God *forced* people to obey him, we would simply be puppets. There would be no real relationship between us and God. And God still wants that relationship. He wants us to obey him out of respect and love—not because it is required.

○ ○ ○ ○ ○ ○ ○ ○ ○ ● ○ ○ ○ ○ ○ ○ ○ ○ ○ ○ ● ○ ○ ○ ○ ○

*Today I have given you the choice between life and death, between blessings and curses. . . . You can make this choice by loving the Lord your God, obeying him, and committing yourself firmly to him. This is the key to your life.* DEUTERONOMY 30:19-20

# Q. WHO CONVINCED EVE TO EAT THE FRUIT?

*Did she really listen to a talking snake?*

A. Yes, Eve listened . . . but it wasn't the snake talking. Most experts agree that the voice she heard was coming from Satan himself. He used the serpent to deliver his message to Eve, and unfortunately, she listened.

There are other instances of animals talking that are recorded in the Bible. The most well-known example is when Balaam's donkey spoke to him in Numbers 22. Another interesting thing is that Eve didn't seem to consider it strange that the snake was speaking. We don't know what the first animals were like or what they could or could not do.

The important part of this story is that Eve (and Adam) listened to the snake (Satan) and disobeyed God. This began the reality of sin for all people since Adam and Eve's children inherited this tendency toward disobedience, and humans have been dealing with a sinful nature ever since.

○ ○ ○ ○ ○ ○ ● ○ ○ ● ○ ○ ○ ○ ○ ○ ● ○ ○ ● ● ● ○ ○ ● ○ ○ ○ ○ ● ● ○

*The serpent was the shrewdest of all the wild animals the LORD God had made. One day he asked the woman, "Did God really say you must not eat the fruit from any of the trees in the garden?"*

GENESIS 3:1

## Q. DID ADAM AND EVE ACTUALLY TAKE A BITE OF AN APPLE?

*How do we know it was an apple and not a pear or some other kind of fruit?*

A. When artists illustrate the story of the first sin, they often show Eve biting into an apple from the tree. Maybe that's because an apple is a familiar fruit. But the truth is that we don't know what kind of fruit Eve picked from the tree of the knowledge of good and evil. The Bible just calls it "fruit." Maybe Eve ate a pomegranate or a fig, or maybe she bit into a fruit that doesn't exist anymore. What we do know is that it must have looked delicious because Eve wanted to taste it.

We also know that the fruit from that tree is the only food in the Garden of Eden that Adam and Eve were forbidden to eat. They had one rule. Just one. And they broke it. At that moment sin entered their hearts, and everything changed for humankind.

*The LORD God warned him, "You may freely eat the fruit of every tree in the garden— except the tree of the knowledge of good and evil. If you eat its fruit, you are sure to die."*

GENESIS 2:16-17

# Q. WHY DID ADAM AND EVE HAVE TO LEAVE THE GARDEN?

*If God made the Garden of Eden just for them, why did he make them leave?*

A. God gave Adam and Eve one rule. They were not to eat the fruit from the tree in the center of the Garden. The punishment for breaking that one rule would be death.

God didn't mean that they would drop dead the instant they tasted the fruit. Scripture shows us that they didn't. The death they experienced was separation from God, the built-in consequence of sin. Immediately after Adam and Eve disobeyed God, they began to hide from him to create distance. They could no longer live in intimate trust with their Creator. God followed through by sending them away from the Garden so they wouldn't eat from the "tree of life" and live forever in a sinful state.

This separation from God has been passed to all humankind. Every one of us still struggles with the urge to hide from God and choose our own way instead of his. But remember, God did not abandon Adam and Eve after they left the Garden. And because of Jesus' death and resurrection, we can once again have a personal relationship with God.

- - - - - - - - - - - - - - - - - - - - - - - - - -

*Look, the human beings have become like us, knowing both good and evil. What if they reach out, take fruit from the tree of life, and eat it? Then they will live forever!* GENESIS 3:22

# Q. DO ANIMALS HAVE SPIRITS?

*Will my pet be in heaven with me someday?*

A. Our pets are gifts from God, aren't they? They bring such joy and comfort. Many people have wondered whether they will see their beloved pets again in heaven. But do animals have souls like humans do? After all, people are created in God's image, and animals are not. So will there be animals in heaven?

In the Bible, the book of Isaiah describes animals that are natural enemies on earth—such as lions and lambs—living peacefully together in heaven. And John's visions of heaven recorded in Revelation include beautiful white horses. So yes, it's reasonable to believe there will be animals in heaven.

Will your specific dog or cat or parakeet be there? In all honesty, we have no proof of that. But it makes sense that God wants heaven to be filled with joy and love. If that means having your beloved pet with you, then it's quite possible it will happen.

*In that day the wolf and the lamb will live together; the leopard will lie down with the baby goat. The calf and the yearling will be safe with the lion, and a little child will lead them all.*

ISAIAH 11:6

# Q. WHAT IS OUR RESPONSIBILITY FOR GOD'S CREATION?

*Does God command that we take care of creation?*

A. From the very beginning, God instructed human beings to care for his creation. Adam and Eve were given the job of taking care of the Garden of Eden. God also told them to "rule" over the earth and the animals. But "rule" doesn't mean to exploit or destroy. Good rulers are supposed to take care of what they rule over, not use it for selfish reasons.

Remember, God made everything in the world. He said it was good. He was happy with his creation. The world belongs to God, not to human beings. So the job of taking care of creation is an act of obedience and responsibility to God. It is also a gift to other people, especially those who may not know God yet, because God often reveals himself through his creation.

So our responsibility is to respect, honor, and care for what God made. In practical terms, this could mean anything from crop rotation to pollution controls to not littering. Our specific responsibility is something to be determined in prayer and careful listening.

*The LORD God placed the man in the Garden of Eden to tend and watch over it.* GENESIS 2:15

Faith shows the reality
of what we hope for;
it is the evidence
of things
we cannot see.

Hebrews 11:1

# Part 3

# QUESTIONS AND ANSWERS
# ABOUT THE BIBLE

# Q. WHAT IS THE BIBLE? WHY IS IT IMPORTANT?

*Is it necessary for me to read and study it?*

A. The Bible is called God's Word because God inspired the people who wrote it to record his messages, commands, and stories for people to read and learn from. The Bible tells the centuries-old story of God's interaction with his people. It also answers questions about how to live, how to treat others, how to know God, and how to live for him.

The Bible has survived for thousands of years in spite of efforts to destroy it. God has always protected it so that his message has never been lost.

It is important to read and study the Bible because it teaches us about God and ourselves. Most people find they can read and study it every day and still keep learning new things. The effort put into studying the Bible pays off as we gain a better understanding of God and ourselves and a closer relationship with him.

° ° ° ° ° ° ° ° °° ° ° ° ° ° ° ° ° ° ° ° ° ° ° ° ° ° ° ° °

*The word of God is alive and powerful. It is sharper than the sharpest two-edged sword, cutting between soul and spirit, between joint and marrow. It exposes our innermost thoughts and desires.* HEBREWS 4:12

## Q. ARE THE BIBLE AND THE WORD OF GOD THE SAME THING?

*Are there two different books to study to know what God wants me to know?*

A. The Bible and the Word of God are the same thing. The word *Bible* comes from the ancient Greek word *biblia*, which means "book." *Biblia* eventually became *Bible* in the English language. The word *holy* was added to the title because the Bible is an important book of faith.

The Bible is often referred to by other terms as well. Some people refer to it as *Scripture*—from the Latin word for "writings." And the Bible is also called the Word of God ("the Word" for short) because Christians believe that it contains God's message to humankind, written down for all people to read.

Interestingly enough, the book of John also uses the term *Word* to refer to Jesus—and in many English versions it also says that when Jesus became human, the Word "became flesh." This is a poetic way of saying that Jesus was God's ultimate communication with the world.

° ° ° ° ° • ° ° ° ° ° ° ° ° ° ° ° • ° ° ° ° ° ° ° ° ° °

*The commandments of the LORD are right, bringing joy to the heart. The commands of the LORD are clear, giving insight for living.* PSALM 19:8

## Q. WHY DID GOD GIVE US THE BIBLE?

*What did he want us to absorb from it?*

A. God gave us the Bible because he loves us. The Bible tells us that we are sinners who cannot have a relationship with God or enter his heaven without understanding that truth. But the Bible also tells us how diligently our loving God has worked through the entire course of human history to remedy that problem. Eventually he sent his own Son, Jesus, to earth to save us—and the Bible tells that story too.

The Bible explains how to obey God, serve him, and love him. He wants us to understand how to live with others and care for them. He also wants us to understand that there is no hope of an eternity spent with him if we do not accept Jesus. All of this is outlined in the Bible.

*People do not live by bread alone, but by every word that comes from the mouth of God.* MATTHEW 4:4

# Q. IS THERE ANY EVIDENCE THE BIBLE IS TRUE EXCEPT IN THE BIBLE ITSELF?

*Bible verses can't be used to prove the Bible is true, so how do I know I can trust its integrity?*

A. It's true you won't find scientific or historical proof for everything you read in the Bible. The Bible goes back too far in time for that, and it isn't meant for historical or scientific purposes alone.

But there *is* archaeological evidence that affirms that certain events recorded in the Old Testament actually happened. Some archaeologists even state that they do their research with the Bible in hand because it supports their findings. Many events of the New Testament have also been documented by outside sources. The Jewish historian Josephus verified that Jesus lived and that many people followed him. Several Roman observers also wrote about the early church in ways that verified the New Testament accounts.

There's another kind of outside evidence that many find compelling: changed lives. Spending time in the Bible and living with faith make people different. That difference is clearly visible in their lives—another reason to trust the truth found in the Bible.

*Truth springs up from the earth, and righteousness smiles down from heaven.* PSALM 85:11

## Q. CAN I TRUST WHAT THE BIBLE SAYS?

*How can I know that God meant all the things he said in the Bible?*

A. The starting point for trusting the Bible is to have faith that God exists. Without faith, it will be difficult to believe what the Bible says. Test the Bible by studying God's Word. Then pray, believing he will answer. See how God responds.

When you try to live by the standards God has outlined in the Bible, you'll find that you get along better with most people. You will have more peace in your life as you learn that you can trust God to take care of you and guide you. So your own personal history with the Bible is the best way to know you can trust it. But it also helps to listen to how other people describe God's work in their lives. That way you can share mutual encouragement and build one another's faith.

* * *

*Lead me by your truth and teach me, for you are the God who saves me. All day long I put my hope in you.*  PSALM 25:5

## Q. WHO WROTE THE BIBLE?

*There are so many individual books and chapters in the Bible. Did one person write them all?*

A. God is the ultimate author of the Bible. The book of 2 Timothy says all Scripture is "inspired by God"—the translated phrase literally means "God-breathed." But the actual words of Scripture—often consisting of stories that had been passed down orally for many years—were preserved by at least forty different writers over many centuries. Some lived before Jesus was on earth, and others were contemporaries of Jesus and witnessed his miracles and teachings. Still others lived after Jesus rose from the dead. Different writers addressed different audiences—for example, the nation of Israel before Jesus came, the tribes of Judah and Benjamin after their return from captivity, and other nations outside of Israel. Many wrote letters that eventually became books in the Bible. Some wrote down their dreams and visions.

God made sure that the individual writing styles of these people were preserved, even when they recorded the same events. As a result, the Bible reads like a rich collection of literature—stories, poems, teaching, letters—all full of useful wisdom about God.

○ ○ ○ ○ ○ ○ ● ○ ○ ○ ○ ○ ○ ○ ○ ○ ○ ○ ● ● ○ ○ ○ ○ ○ ○ ○ ○ ○ ○

*All Scripture is inspired by God and is useful to teach us what is true. . . . It corrects us when we are wrong and teaches us to do what is right.* 2 TIMOTHY 3:16

# Q. WHEN WAS THE BIBLE WRITTEN?

*I know it's very old. How is it still applicable to me today?*

A. The earlier parts of the Bible were written nearly thirty-five hundred years ago, and the newer parts around nineteen hundred years ago. Yes, that's a long time, but the truth of the message in the Bible has not changed—nor will it ever.

Tradition holds that the first five books of the Bible, which tell the story of God's earliest dealings with the Hebrew people, were written by Moses, who also played an important part in the events described in those books. The most recent book in the Bible, the book of Revelation, was written by the apostle John, one of Jesus' twelve disciples, around AD 95.

God is timeless. In fact, time really means nothing to him because he is eternal. So the truths God shared through the words of Scripture are constantly relevant to our lives and the choices we make. Even though the Bible was written a long time ago, it is still as meaningful today as it ever was.

- - - - - - - - - - - - - - - - - - - - - - - - - - -

*Such things were written in the Scriptures long ago to teach us. And the Scriptures give us hope and encouragement as we wait patiently for God's promises to be fulfilled.* ROMANS 15:4

# Q. IN WHAT LANGUAGE WAS THE BIBLE WRITTEN?

*Was it written in several languages or just one?*

A. Most of the Old Testament was written in ancient Hebrew. The ancient Hebrew alphabet had twenty-two consonants and no written vowels! Although ancient and modern Hebrew aren't identical, Hebrew-speaking people today can recognize the words that were used. A small portion of the Old Testament was written in Aramaic, which is similar to ancient Hebrew. It is probably also the language that Jesus spoke.

Although educated Jewish men still spoke Hebrew, the New Testament was written in Greek because it was the most widespread language in the Roman Empire at the time.

The Bible was written so that it could be understood by the people reading it and hearing it at the time. Thankfully, scholars and translators have also made it understandable to people who live in our time!

- - - - - - - - - - - - - - - - - - - - - - - - - -

*Your word is a lamp to guide my feet and a light for my path.*
PSALM 119:105

## Q. WHY ARE THERE SO MANY DIFFERENT KINDS OF BIBLES?

*How can I know which one is best?*

A. Very few of us can read the Bible in its original languages. So we are blessed to have many different translations of the Bible available to us.

The best way to know which translation is most helpful for you is to choose a verse or two and look them up in different versions to compare. You can do this at a bookstore or online at sites such as BibleGateway.com. See which version makes sense to you and is easy to read and understand. Ask your friends and your pastor, if you have one.

It is actually a good idea to have more than one translation handy to compare stories and verses in order to make sure you get a good understanding of what God is saying. A few recommended translations are the New Living Translation (used in this book), the English Standard Version, and the New International Version, but there are many that are helpful.

*It is the same with my word. I send it out, and it always produces fruit. It will accomplish all I want it to, and it will prosper everywhere I send it.* ISAIAH 55:11

# Q. WHY DO I KEEP HEARING ABOUT "BOOKS OF THE BIBLE"?

*Isn't it just one big book?*

A. The Bible consists of many shorter sections we call "books." They were recorded at different times by many people and contain different kinds of material. Some of the books tell stories and narratives. Some feature poetry, songs, and sayings. Some are books of prophecy addressed to God's people, and some are letters to specific groups.

All in all, there are sixty-six books in the Bible. All sixty-six of these books together give us a good understanding of God's teachings and how he relates to people, both past and present. God loves us so much that he wants to be sure we understand his love.

It's important to understand that all of these books were not originally written as part of a whole but were later put together in one volume. By the year 1600, Bibles had also been divided into chapters and verses for the sake of convenience, making certain passages easier to find.

*Praise the LORD, all you nations. Praise him, all you people of the earth. For his unfailing love for us is powerful; the LORD's faithfulness endures forever. Praise the LORD!* PSALM 117:1-2

# Q. WHAT IS A TESTAMENT?

*Why is the Bible divided into an old one and a new one?*

A. The word *testament* means "covenant" or "agreement." It is the word used to describe the two main parts of the Christian Bible.

The Old Testament, sometimes called the Hebrew Scriptures, tells the story of God's ongoing covenant with the Israelite people (also called Hebrews) and his relationship with them over thousands of years. Today's Jewish people, who also honor these Scriptures as sacred, descend from the Israelites. The Old Testament is made up of thirty-nine books written by various authors.

The New Testament tells the story of a new covenant God made with Israel, and ultimately all of humanity, by sending his Son, Jesus, into the world. Written by a variety of Jesus' followers after his death and resurrection, it is the basis of the Christian faith. It consists of twenty-seven books.

○ ○ ● ○ ○ ● ○ ○ ○ ● ● ○ ○ ○ ○ ● ○ ○ ○ ○ ○ ● ○ ○ ○ ● ○ ○

*This is the everlasting covenant: I will always be your God and the God of your descendants after you.*   GENESIS 17:7

# Q. WHAT IS IN THE OLD TESTAMENT?

*How does it relate to the New Testament?*

A. The Old Testament is basically the story of how God started the world and interacted with his chosen people. One of the central events of this story is the Exodus, when Moses led the Israelites out of slavery in Egypt to a new homeland that God had promised them.

Another prominent feature of the Old Testament is that it spells out God's law—his guidelines for living. The Old Testament also contains some beautiful poetry, including a book of hymns and prayers called the Psalms. Christians through the ages have used the Psalms to voice their own thoughts and feelings to God.

Finally, the Old Testament contains books of prophecy—messages God sent to his people. Many of these warn of the consequences of sin, and some tell of a coming Messiah—a promised deliverer of God's people. These "messianic" prophecies were fulfilled in the events of Jesus' life on earth more than two thousand years ago, and they also foretell his future return to physically rule and reign on earth.

* * *

*I tell you the truth, until heaven and earth disappear, not even the smallest detail of God's law will disappear until its purpose is achieved.* MATTHEW 5:18

# Q. WHAT IS IN THE NEW TESTAMENT?

*How is it different from the Old Testament?*

A. The New Testament is the newer section of the Bible. It focuses primarily on the life and teachings of Jesus and the early days of the church. Christians believe the New Testament confirms the message of the Old Testament and illustrates how Jesus fulfilled its prophecies of a coming Messiah who would bring salvation and establish God's Kingdom.

The first four books, the Gospels, are essentially biographies of Jesus. They record his earthly life, teachings, and miracles and are named after the four disciples who are traditionally attributed with writing them: Matthew, Mark, Luke, and John.

The book of Acts picks up the story after Jesus' resurrection and chronicles how the church got started and grew. After that come the Epistles, which are actually letters written to encourage and teach Christians in various New Testament—era churches. Finally, the book of Revelation records a vision Jesus' disciple John experienced. This book includes prophecy about the end times, when God's judgment will fall on unbelievers and a beautiful new heaven and new earth will be established.

*"The day is coming," says the Lord, "when I will make a new covenant with the people of Israel and Judah."* JEREMIAH 31:31

# Q. WHY SHOULD I STUDY THE OLD TESTAMENT?

*Isn't the New Testament more relevant to life today?*

A. In the first place, Jesus himself studied the Hebrew Scriptures. That's reason enough for us to do it too. But there are other reasons as well.

The Old Testament confirms the New Testament. It reveals that God is the Creator of everything and that he is in control. The Old Testament shows how much God loves his people, guiding and protecting them through the centuries. The Old Testament also establishes God's laws so that people have a foundation for how to live.

The Old Testament reveals that even after Adam and Eve sinned, God had a plan that would make it possible for people to have a personal relationship with him and be a part of his family. It also prophesied the coming of Jesus, which changed everything. There is now a new covenant—a new deal between humankind and God—because Jesus paid for our sins. But that doesn't mean the Old Testament isn't valuable. It gives a fuller meaning to the New Testament.

*Remember the things I have done in the past. For I alone am God! I am God, and there is none like me.*   ISAIAH 46:9

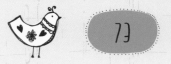

# Q. WHAT ARE THE DEAD SEA SCROLLS?

*Why are they important?*

A. The Dead Sea Scrolls are a large collection of Jewish documents discovered in caves near the Dead Sea in Israel. Back in 1947, a simple shepherd was looking for a lost goat. He tossed a rock into a cave and heard it hit something—a ceramic jar that contained leather and papyrus scrolls. After that, many other scrolls were found in nearby caves. The collection as a whole contains portions of every book in the Hebrew Bible except the book of Esther!

These scrolls are important because they are more than two thousand years old and are the oldest known copies of any Scripture—older than any discovered before. Their existence helps prove the consistency and protection of God's Word through the centuries.

∘ ∘ ∘ ∘ ∘ ∘ ∘ ∘ ∘ ∙ ∘ ∙ ∘ ∘ ∘ ∘ ∘ ∘ ∘ ∘ ∘ ∙ ∘ ∘ ∘ ∘ ∘ ∘

*Heaven and earth will disappear, but my words will never disappear.* MATTHEW 24:35

## Q. HOW WERE THE BOOKS OF THE BIBLE CHOSEN?

*Were there some books written that didn't get included in the "final" version?*

A. The most important thing to remember is that God is the one who guided the final decision. He did this by working through churches and various groups and gatherings called councils. Their experience and God's inspiration narrowed down what would be included in the "canon"—the official collection of divinely inspired books.

It wasn't too complicated to know which books should be included in the Old Testament. God had guided the Jewish people through that process many years before. The New Testament canon was more of a challenge. The books that were finally chosen met certain criteria:

- The writer was someone who knew Jesus or was in close relationship with someone who did.
- The majority of churches accepted the book.
- The book was consistent with other scriptural teaching.
- Its teachings were composed of high moral and spiritual values that reflected the work of the Holy Spirit.

*The instructions of the LORD are perfect, reviving the soul. The decrees of the LORD are trustworthy, making wise the simple.*

PSALM 19:7

# Q. WHO WROTE THE MOST BOOKS IN THE BIBLE?

*Is one person the "main" author?*

A. This *could* be a trick question because, in a sense, the most prolific author of the Bible is God. But from a human perspective, the hands-down winner would be a man named Paul. This apostle started out as a Jerusalem Jew named Saul, who passionately opposed the new Christian movement and zealously persecuted the followers of Christ.

Following his dramatic conversion to faith in Jesus, however, Saul's name was changed to Paul, and his new passion became sharing the Good News of Jesus with all who would listen. He traveled throughout the Roman Empire planting churches, and when he was away from those churches, he wrote them letters that taught doctrine (spiritual truth) and encouraged church leaders to grow strong in their faith and to work together to spread the gospel. At least thirteen of those letters became books of the Bible.

Not everyone was happy about Paul's missionary efforts. He was arrested more than once and even wrote some of his famous letters from jail. But not even imprisonment and persecution could stop Paul from spreading the gospel. He even told his jailers and fellow inmates about Jesus!

- - - - - - - - - - - - - - - - - - - - - - - -

*Saul stayed with the apostles and went all around Jerusalem with them, preaching boldly in the name of the Lord.* ACTS 9:28

## Q. HOW DID PAUL BECOME A FOLLOWER OF JESUS?

*From persecuting Christians to writing part of the Bible—that's a big change. How exactly did that happen?*

A. The big change happened when Saul was on his way to the city of Damascus to persecute Christians. Suddenly a bright light shone down on him and a voice asked, "Saul! Why are you persecuting me?" It was the voice of Jesus.

Saul fell to the ground, and when he got up, he was blind. His companions guided him on to Damascus, where God had told some Christians to take care of him. (Yes, they were nervous about that!) By the time Saul could see again, he knew that Jesus was real and that he had been wrong to persecute Christians. His name was changed to Paul, and for the rest of his life he lived as a passionate missionary for Jesus.

- - - - - - - - - - - - - - - - - - - - - - - - - - - -

*[Paul wrote to Timothy:] As for me, my life has already been poured out as an offering to God. . . . I have fought the good fight, I have finished the race, and I have remained faithful. And now the prize awaits me—the crown of righteousness, which the Lord, the righteous Judge, will give me on the day of his return.* 2 TIMOTHY 4:6-8

## Q. WHAT IS THE EASIEST WAY TO GET STARTED READING THE BIBLE?

*Should I start at the beginning and read all the way to the end?*

A. If you are just beginning to read the Bible, it's probably not the best idea to start with the book of Genesis and read straight through. Since the Bible is actually a collection of books written in different styles, it does not read smoothly from beginning to end.

A better strategy is to begin with one of the four Gospels—Matthew, Mark, Luke, or John. Those books, found at the beginning of the New Testament, will introduce you to Jesus and his teachings. Mark is a nice place to start because it will give you a quick overview of Jesus' ministry. The Gospel of John is also good because of its special focus on God's incredible love. From one of those starting points, you can move to other places in the Bible—Genesis and Exodus for great stories about the early years of God's people, Psalms and Proverbs for wisdom and inspiration, Romans and 1 Corinthians for basic instruction in Christian truth . . . and onward from there.

*Like newborn babies, you must crave pure spiritual milk so that you will grow into a full experience of salvation. Cry out for this nourishment.*   1 PETER 2:2

# Q. HOW CAN I FIND CERTAIN PASSAGES IN THE BIBLE?

*What if I'm given a specific verse to look up or I'm looking for verses on a specific topic—how can I find them?*

A. Remember, the Bible is divided into books, and in most translations each book is divided into chapters and verses. If someone suggests that you look up John 3:16, you can check the table of contents to find the book of John, then flip through it until you find chapter 3 and verse 16. With practice, you'll begin to have a feel for where the books are found without having to check the contents. You can also use an online Bible such as BibleGateway.com to search for specific Scriptures.

But what if you're looking for a particular topic, not a specific passage or verse? Then you need a concordance, which lists verses by topics like love, forgiveness, judgment, and many others. Many Bibles include one of these. You might also find it helpful to get a study Bible, ask a friend, or consult a reliable online source. And don't forget to ask the Holy Spirit to direct you through your reading.

*Everyone who asks, receives. Everyone who seeks, finds. And to everyone who knocks, the door will be opened.* LUKE 11:10

# Q. ARE THERE ERRORS OR CONTRADICTIONS IN THE BIBLE?

*Some passages don't seem to be in line with others I've read. Is the Bible consistent?*

A. Some parts of the Bible do seem to contradict other parts. But remember, the Bible is a collection of manuscripts written over thousands of years by at least forty writers from various backgrounds and cultures. They viewed situations from different vantage points, wrote to people in a variety of circumstances, and wrote in a wide range of styles—poetry, symbolic language, stories, even lists. Given that reality, the message of the Bible is surprisingly consistent.

The varying perspectives in the Bible can actually be an advantage. For example, the four writers who told the story of Jesus' life wrote for different purposes and audiences and therefore included different details. The result is a fuller, truer picture of what happened and what it meant.

If you come across something in the Bible that seems to be confusing or contradictory, don't be afraid to look into it more deeply. You can do your own study, using materials written by dependable sources. You might also want to talk to a respected pastor or Bible teacher.

○ ◦ ○ ◦ ○ ◦ ○ ◦ • ○ ◦ ○ ◦ ◦ ○ ○ ◦ ○ ○ ◦ ○ ○ ◦ ○ ◦

*The very essence of your words is truth; all your just regulations will stand forever.* PSALM 119:160

# Q. DO SCIENCE AND THE BIBLE DISAGREE?

*Some scientists say that the Bible is totally untrue. There seems to be difficulty in bringing the teachings of the Bible and science together. How can I believe something that science doesn't support?*

A. Yes, to be honest, there are contradictions between what the Bible says and what many (not all) scientists believe about how everything began, how it works, and how it will end. On the other hand, new scientific discoveries often support the biblical record in surprising ways, and plenty of scientists are also Christian believers.

What is most important to understand is that the Bible was never meant to be a scientific textbook. Its purpose is to share the deeper truth about who made the world and why—and what it all means for how we live. Christian believers through the centuries, and today, have found this truth to be dependable and life giving.

Our universe is a complex and amazing thing. A Christian should respect science and appreciate how it can further explain what God has revealed in the Bible, but belief in science should never supersede God's truth.

○ ○ ○ ○ ○ ● ○ ○ ○ ○ ○ ○ ○ ○ ● ○ ○ ● ● ● ○ ○ ○ ○ ○ ○ ● ○ ○

*The heavens proclaim the glory of God. The skies display his craftsmanship.* PSALM 19:1

# Q. WHERE CAN I FIND STORIES ABOUT JESUS IN THE BIBLE?

*I want to know about his life and teachings. Which parts should I read?*

A. The first four books of the New Testament (often called the Gospels) are the best places to read about Jesus. Of course, Jesus is present in the rest of the Bible, too, but these four Gospels tell the story of his ministry on earth, including his death and resurrection. Tradition holds that each Gospel was written by the person the book is named for. Each presents the story from a different perspective:

- Matthew looks back at Old Testament prophecies, emphasizing that Jesus is the fulfillment of those prophecies and is the Messiah the Jewish people have been waiting for.
- Mark provides a dynamic, condensed story of what happened in Jesus' life.
- Luke shares the beautiful story of Jesus' birth and emphasizes his love and compassion for people during his lifetime.
- John explores the meaning of Jesus' life, death, and resurrection and emphasizes that Jesus is both God and human.

Together, the four Gospels offer a more complete story of Jesus' life and work.

*This is the Good News about Jesus the Messiah, the Son of God.*

MARK 1:1

# Q. WHAT DOES "GOSPEL" MEAN?

*And why are the first four books in the New Testament called Gospels?*

A. The word *gospel* actually means "good news." The Good News is the story of Jesus. But to understand why this news is good, you must first understand what the bad news is. The bad news is that all people are lost, hopelessly corrupted by their sin. This condition separates them from God and condemns them to eternity in hell—away from God.

The Good News is that Jesus came to earth, taught about God, died for the sins of humanity, and was raised back to life by God. In the process, he defeated death and made a way for us to be saved from our crippling, chronic sin. By accepting Jesus as Savior, we are reconnected to God and have the blessing of his Spirit living in us—strengthening, guiding, protecting, and loving us. We also have the promise of eternity in heaven with God.

So why are certain books of the Bible called Gospels? Simply because by telling the story of Jesus, they are also sharing the Good News.

*Jesus traveled through all the towns and villages . . . teaching in the synagogues and announcing the Good News about the Kingdom.* MATTHEW 9:35

## Q. HOW CAN THE BIBLE HELP ME?

*What difference will it make in my life?*

A. Life can be hard. Everyone has struggles, sorrow, and grief. Everyone has anxiety and questions about how to obey God and how to treat other people. The Bible helps answer those questions. More important, it points toward the One who is the ultimate Answer.

Many people who have spent a lot of time in the Bible say that you don't read the Bible; it reads you. In other words, the Bible helps us understand ourselves better and look at our lives more honestly. It shows us how to live better and how to draw closer to God. It helps us face our grief and frustration and express our joy and thankfulness. Even though it was written thousands of years ago, the Bible is, in a sense, a personal message from God to you. The more you read and study it, the clearer that message will be.

° ○ ○ ○ ○ ○ ○ ○ ● ● ● ○ ○ ○ ○ ○ ○ ○ ○ ○ ● ○ ○ ○ ○ ○

*You will understand what is right, just, and fair, and you will find the right way to go.* PROVERBS 2:9

## Q. WHY SHOULD I MEMORIZE SCRIPTURE?

*I have my Bible, so why should I make the effort to memorize Bible verses?*

A. Memorizing portions of Scripture is actually one of the most important ways you can grow as a Christian. The Word of God is powerful, so when it is in your mind and heart, its truth will spring to your thoughts at times when you need it—when you are weary, sad, or tempted to sin. Memorized Scripture is your offensive weapon to help you fight off Satan's attacks and get past the roadblocks that keep you from living for God. Even Jesus used Scripture to help him resist Satan. It is also a handy tool to use when you have the opportunity to share God's love. The more verses you have in your memory, the more strength and comfort you will find from God and the more your faith will grow.

Memorizing Scripture isn't hard. Simply find a version of Scripture you understand and can read easily. Then begin learning a passage by heart, one verse at a time. Some people write their verses on index cards or keep them in their phones and carry them around until they've committed them to memory.

*I have hidden your word in my heart, that I might not sin against you.* PSALM 119:11

# Q. WHY DOES GOD HAVE SO MANY NAMES IN THE BIBLE?

*Why didn't people just call him "God"?*

A. Names are more than just personal labels in the Bible. They *mean* something. In biblical times, in fact, people's names often changed after they encountered a significant event. Abram became Abraham, Jacob became Israel, and so on.

God's most common name in the Old Testament is *YHWH*. It was probably pronounced "Yahweh," but we don't know that for sure because it was considered so holy that people almost never said it out loud! *YHWH* comes from the verb meaning "to be," which makes sense because God once told Moses that his name was "I AM." Most Bible translations render this name as LORD (with small capitals). Other Old Testament names for God include *El*, *Elohim*, *Adonai*, and a variety of descriptive combinations like *Yahweh-Rapha* ("The Lord heals").

There are fewer names for God in the Greek New Testament, but they also tell us a lot about both God and the people who said his name. The most common is *theos*, which simply means "God," but there are also *kyrios* (Lord), *despotes* (Master), *Pater* (Father), and the intimate Aramaic word *Abba*, which basically means "Daddy."

_ _ _ _ _ _ _ _ _ _ _ _ _ _ _ _ _ _ _ _ _ _ _ _ _

*God replied to Moses, "I AM WHO I AM. Say this to the people of Israel: I AM has sent me to you."* EXODUS 3:14

# Q. WHY WERE GOD'S PEOPLE CALLED THE ISRAELITES?

*How is an Israelite different from a Hebrew or a Jew?*

A. *Hebrew, Israelite,* and *Jew* all refer to descendants of Abraham, whose story is told in the book of Genesis. Abraham and his children were known as Hebrews until his grandson Jacob wrestled with an angel and got a new name—Israel. After that, the Hebrews were also called Israelites or the children of Israel.

There were twelve tribes of Israelites, each led by a son of Jacob, and over time they were divided into two larger groups. The ten northern tribes started calling themselves by the collective name of Israel, and the southern tribes, who took the name Judah, began calling themselves Jews. Both Israel and Judah were taken captive by foreign powers, but only those who were originally from Judah (like the family Jesus would descend from) returned from captivity, and since then they have been known as the Jews. By New Testament times, the terms *Hebrew, Israelite,* and *Jew* were sometimes used interchangeably to refer to descendants of Abraham.

- - - - - - - - - - - - - - - - - - - - - - - -

*"Your name will no longer be Jacob,"* the man told him. *"From now on you will be called Israel, because you have fought with God and with men and have won."* GENESIS 32:28

# Q. WHY WERE THE ISRAELITES GOD'S CHOSEN PEOPLE?

*What purpose did he choose them for?*

A. The Bible makes it clear that the Israelites were special to God. He rescued them from slavery and starvation, taught them how to act, gave them a place to live, warned them when they went astray, and gave them both love and loving discipline through the years. But why did God focus on just one people?

The Bible itself answers that question. God chose the people of Israel to be a blessing to the entire world. When he made his original covenant or "deal" with Abraham, his idea was to focus on one family and grow them into a nation that would "infect" the rest of the world with God's goodness.

When God sent his Son, Jesus, into the world through Mary, a descendant of Abraham, God fulfilled that promise. Jesus came to redeem Israel and all of humanity from their evil practices, self-righteousness, and thoughtless selfishness. The world is still in the process of receiving that blessing, and one day everything will be made right when Jesus returns to rule and reign on the earth.

*The LORD had said to Abram, . . . "I will make you into a great nation. I will bless you and make you famous, and you will be a blessing to others. . . . All the families on earth will be blessed through you."* GENESIS 12:1-3

## Q. HOW DID THE ISRAELITES END UP AS SLAVES IN EGYPT?

*I know Moses led them out of Egypt. But how did they get there in the first place?*

A. Some of Abraham's great-grandsons were jealous of their brother Joseph because he was their father's favorite son. They sold him to foreigners, and Joseph was taken to Egypt and sold into slavery. After much suffering and through miraculous circumstances, he became the assistant to Egypt's ruler (Pharaoh). When famine struck, Joseph stored up provisions and sent for his family.

For generations the Israelites prospered in Egypt, but in time a new Pharaoh rose to power who knew nothing about Joseph and enslaved the Israelites. But God worked through Moses to perform miracles that freed his people. Moses led them out of Egypt and toward the land that God had promised Abraham.

God's view of time is different from ours. It's easy to assume he's dragging his feet when actually he's arranging events for our good. The story of Abraham's descendants is a good lesson in patience and trusting God over the long haul.

*Your descendants will be strangers in a foreign land, where they will be oppressed as slaves.... After four generations your descendants will return here to this land.* GENESIS 15:13, 16

## Q. WHY DID THE ISRAELITES HAVE TO SPEND FORTY YEARS IN THE DESERT?

*It's not that far from Egypt to the Promised Land. Why did it take them so long to get there?*

A. The main reason the Israelites had to wander for forty years was their own disobedience and lack of faith.

When they approached the Promised Land, Moses sent twelve spies to check it out. They searched the land for forty days. Ten of them came back fearful that they couldn't conquer the giant people who lived there. Two argued that they had God on their side, so they could do anything. But the people listened to the fearful spies, even though they had just witnessed amazing miracles performed on their behalf.

Since the people chose not to trust God to keep his word and give them the land, God sent them back into the wilderness to wander some more. The sentence was forty years—one year for each day the spies had explored the land. Meanwhile the entire generation of disobedient people died, except for the two faithful spies—Joshua and Caleb. Only then were the people allowed to enter the land.

*It is impossible to please God without faith. Anyone who wants to come to him must believe that God exists and that he rewards those who sincerely seek him.* HEBREWS 11:6

90

## Q. WHY IS THERE SO MUCH KILLING IN THE OLD TESTAMENT?

*More important, why does God seem okay with it?*

A. The Old Testament *is* kind of a bloody book. There were many wars, and the losers were often treated with great cruelty. God even commanded his people to wipe out entire nations. How could a loving God do that?

This has bothered Christians for many centuries. But it might help to consider certain realities. First, many of those nations, like the Canaanites, practiced such evil things as child sacrifice, incest, and murder. They also worshiped idols. God wanted to keep his people from being contaminated by false religions and heathen cultures.

Second, we have accounts of people among those nations, such as Rahab of Jericho, who *did* turn to God and were saved. So it's possible that not *everyone* in these countries was slaughtered after all. But the most important thing to remember is that God always makes a way for those who turn to him to be saved.

○ ○ ○ ○ ○ ● ○ ○ ○ ○ ● ○ ○ ○ ● ○ ○ ● ● ● ○ ○ ○ ○ ○ ○ ● ○ ○

*God is both kind and severe. He is severe toward those who disobeyed, but kind to you if you continue to trust in his kindness.* ROMANS 11:22

## Q. WHAT ARE THE TEN COMMANDMENTS?

*Can they help me in my everyday life?*

A. The Ten Commandments (listed in Exodus 20:1-17 and Deuteronomy 5:7-21) are ten rules for how to live in peace with God and others. They're a good basic model for living the way God wants. God gave them to Moses to share with the Israelites, who seemed to have recurring troubles remembering to obey and trust him. The Ten Commandments essentially condense more than six hundred commands given in the Old Testament. The first four commandments are about our relationship to God, and the last six are about our relationships with others. This is what they teach:

1. Don't worship any other god.
2. Don't have any idols.
3. Don't misuse God's name.
4. Remember God's Sabbath day of rest and keep it holy.
5. Honor your father and mother.
6. Do not murder.
7. Do not commit adultery.
8. Do not steal.
9. Do not tell lies about others.
10. Do not covet what someone else has.

*If you love me, obey my commandments.* JOHN 14:15

## Q. WHO WAS KING DAVID, AND HOW WAS HE CONNECTED TO JESUS?

*Why is Jesus called the Son of David? And why does that matter?*

A. David was the second king of Israel, the great but imperfect warrior/poet who composed many of the songs contained in the book of Psalms. David was also the ancestor of Jesus, which is one reason Jesus is referred to several times in the New Testament as the Son of David. In Bible times, *son* didn't just mean a male child of the next generation. It could also mean "coming from."

The fact that Jesus descended from David was very important to Jews of his day. They were waiting for a prophesied Messiah who would restore and redeem Israel, and Old Testament prophecies said that this Messiah would be a descendant of King David.

Of course, Jesus turned out to be a very different kind of Messiah from what the Jews were expecting. He was actually God in human form, and he came for all people, not just Jews. The Son of David turned out to be the Savior of the world—good news for everyone.

*I, Jesus, . . . am both the source of David and the heir to his throne. I am the bright morning star.*   REVELATION 22:16

## Q. WHAT ARE PSALMS?

*Why do people like to read them?*

A. Psalms are songs and prayers that the Israelites used to express their relationship with God. The book of Psalms in the Bible contains 150 of them, many of which were written by David, the second king of Israel.

Psalms fall into different categories. Some, such as Psalm 8, are hymns, intended to be sung in worship. A significant number were written to be performed for royalty. Some are expressions of lament (Psalm 3) or thanksgiving (Psalm 100), and some convey wisdom (Psalm 1).

Many people use the book of Psalms as a guide to personal devotion and prayer. They enjoy the Psalms for their words of comfort, wisdom, and praise. Many also find that these beautiful poems help them express their feelings and draw closer to God.

∘ ∘ ∘ ∘ ∘ ∘ ∘ ∘ ∘ ∘ ∘ ∘ ∘ ∘ ∘ ∘ ∘ ∘ ∘ ∘ ∘ ∘ ∘ ∘ ∘

*Shout with joy to the LORD, all the earth! Worship the LORD with gladness. Come before him, singing with joy.*   PSALM 100:1-2

## Q. WHERE CAN I FIND COMFORT IN THE BIBLE?

*I just need to know that someone cares—someone who is stronger than I am.*

A. The Bible is filled with assurances of God's love and care. A good way to find passages about comfort is by using a concordance, which lists Bible verses that apply to specific topics. Many Bibles have a concordance in the back, so it's easy to look up words such as *care, comfort, love,* or *peace.*

The book of Psalms is a great place to go for comfort. Throughout the ages, men and women have found solace in praying through the beautiful words of these ancient hymns. Psalm 23 is a favorite of many who seek comfort. Whatever you might be feeling—anger, despair, grief—you will find something in the Psalms you can relate to. And many Psalms are structured to help you express your feelings honestly but then gradually find your way back to trusting and thanking God.

The ultimate source of comfort, of course, is the reality of Jesus' death and resurrection. He died for you, taking the punishment for your sin, because he loves you. In rising from the grave, he defeated death. He has promised to be with us always. What could be more comforting than that?

○ ○ ○ ○ ○ ○ ○ ○ ○ ○ ○ ○ ○ ○ ○ ○ ○ ○ ○ ○ ○ ○ ○ ○ ○ ○ ○

*Give your burdens to the LORD, and he will take care of you.*

PSALM 55:22

## Q. WHERE CAN I FIND STORIES IN THE BIBLE ABOUT THE WORLD'S BEGINNINGS?

*Is there a detailed story of how things started?*

A. Genesis, the first book in the Bible, tells the story of the early days of history.

The creation of the world came first. With four simple words, "Let there be light," the universe got its start. Genesis goes on to tell story after fascinating story about God's developing relationship with the people he loved.

After Noah and his family survived the Flood, God promised never to destroy the world by water again. (And he didn't.) And After Abraham and Sarah obeyed God's summons to follow him, he promised they would be parents of a great nation. (They were.) In the process of keeping that promise, God turned a tricky deceiver (Jacob) into a great patriarch (Israel). And he turned the relationship between a bragging little brother (Joseph) and his jealous older brothers into a dramatic story of redemption and rescue.

The pattern of God's faithfulness that we see originating in the book of Genesis later culminates in the coming of Jesus and his offer of redemption to the whole world.

- - - - - - - - - - - - - - - - - - - - - - - -

*[Joseph told his brothers,] "You intended to harm me, but God intended it all for good. He brought me to this position so I could save the lives of many people."* GENESIS 50:20

## Q. WHERE CAN I FIND STORIES IN THE BIBLE ABOUT THE END OF THE WORLD?

*It's kind of scary to think about the world coming to an end. Does God tell us what is going to happen?*

A. Several places in the Bible speak about the end of the world—Daniel 2 and 7–9, Matthew 24, 2 Peter 3, and most of the book of Revelation. All of these descriptions are worth our attention, but there are a few things to keep in mind.

First, it's only the end of the world as we currently know it. A new beginning will follow for those who love God! Second, many of these descriptions are written in highly symbolic language, and not all Christians agree on what they mean. Third, Jesus stressed that no one—not even himself—knows when it's all going to happen, so people who obsess about the end times are probably missing the point. It's more important for us to live faithfully in the meantime than to understand exactly what will happen in the end. And finally, the scary descriptions of the end of the world also bring the ultimate good news: Satan will be defeated. Jesus will return in triumph. There will be no more tears, no more sadness—just a big celebration, and then we will live forever with God.

- - - - - - - - - - - - - - - - - - - - - - - - -

*We are looking forward to the new heavens and new earth he has promised, a world filled with God's righteousness.*

2 PETER 3:13

# Q. WHAT ARE EPISTLES, AND WHY ARE THEY IN THE BIBLE?

*What do we learn from them?*

A. An epistle is a letter. Twenty-two of the twenty-seven books in the New Testament are epistles—letters addressed to groups of Christians or churches in the early days of the church. The epistle is named for either the person who wrote it or the group who received the letter. For instance, the books of 1 and 2 Peter were written by Peter, and the book of Galatians was written by Paul to Christians in a place called Galatia.

Paul wrote thirteen of the Epistles in the Bible. Eight more were written by Jesus' disciples (Peter and John) or family members (James and Jude). No one knows for certain who wrote the letter to the Hebrews.

The Epistles helped shape the early church, and they are still important today. They expand on Jesus' teachings and the reality that all people need a Savior. They also have extensive teachings on how God's people must relate to one another. These letters are in the Bible to encourage readers to stay close to God and serve him wholeheartedly.

*This letter is from Paul, an apostle. I was not appointed by any group of people or any human authority, but by Jesus Christ himself and by God the Father, who raised Jesus from the dead.*

GALATIANS 1:1

## Q. WHERE IN THE BIBLE CAN I FIND GUIDANCE FOR HOW TO LIVE?

*I want to follow God's will. How do I find out what it is?*

A. In a sense, the entire Bible is there for you as a guide for how to live. However, certain parts of the Bible are especially practical and helpful.

Reading about the Ten Commandments is a good place to start. They are a concise summary of God's laws and can be found in Exodus 20:1-17 or Deuteronomy 5:7-21. The book of Proverbs is also full of helpful wisdom. In the New Testament, Jesus' words are essential, especially the Sermon on the Mount found in Matthew 5–7. Paul's epistles and the book of James are great sources of practical advice as well.

But God's guidance in Scripture involves more than just a list of what to do and what not to do. The more you immerse yourself in the entire Bible, the better you will get to know God and understand what he wants. So stay in his Word. Read it, think about it, memorize it, and pay attention to the ways a particular verse speaks into your life in a special way.

God does not make his will a secret. He wants you to be serious about following it and to seek it with your whole heart. The Bible is the best resource to help you do this.

*The LORD will guide you continually, giving you water when you are dry and restoring your strength.* ISAIAH 58:11

## Q. WHAT IS A PROPHET?

*Are there still prophets today?*

A. A prophet isn't necessarily a person who predicts the future; the main function of a prophet is to speak God's truth into the lives of others. However, God may still choose to reveal elements of the future to him or her.

In the Bible, prophets such as Isaiah, Jeremiah, and Ezekiel often were called upon to speak to groups of people and challenge them for disobeying God or misleading God's people. Many times God's prophets were disliked because they called out people who were not obeying God. Being a prophet was not an easy job—but it was an important one.

And yes, there are still prophets today. The ability to prophesy is a spiritual gift from God, and true prophets should be heeded. However, Scripture warns against false prophets who claim to be sharing God's message but actually spread lies. Their words need to be carefully weighed to see whether they are compatible with the entire message of Scripture. It's always wise to be careful whom you listen to.

o o o o o o o o o o o o o o o o o o o o o o o o o o o o

*Dear friends, do not believe everyone who claims to speak by the Spirit. You must test them to see if the spirit they have comes from God. For there are many false prophets in the world.* 1 JOHN 4:1

# Q. WHERE CAN I FIND PROPHECY IN THE BIBLE?

*Is it mostly in the Old Testament, the New Testament, or both?*

A. Prophecy can be found throughout the Bible, but a good place to start is in the last part of the Old Testament. There you'll find the "Major Prophets"—Isaiah, Jeremiah, Lamentations, Ezekiel, and Daniel—plus the twelve shorter "Minor Prophets."

The Old Testament prophets often expressed God's disapproval that his people were neglecting true worship and mistreating the poor, and many warned that punishment was coming. But these prophets also predicted the coming of the Messiah—Jesus—who would redeem and restore God's people. The best-known of these prophecies are found in the book of Isaiah. And the most widely recognized book of prophecy in the New Testament is the last one, Revelation. Some also say that Jesus took a prophetic role in the Gospels by speaking against the powerful religious leaders, warning of future troubles, and predicting God's future reign.

Prophecy is an important part of the Bible, but it can sometimes be difficult to understand. A good set of Bible study tools or a trusted teacher can help you get the most out of your studies.

○ ○ ○ ○ ○ • ○ ○ ○ ○ ○ ○ ○ ○ ○ • ○ • • ○ ○ ○ ○ ○ ○ ○ ○

*Jesus took them through the writings of Moses and all the prophets, explaining from all the Scriptures the things concerning himself.* LUKE 24:27

# Q. HOW CAN I GET THE MOST OUT OF MY SCRIPTURE READING?

*Are there different ways to read and study the Bible?*

A. Even Christians who have been reading the Bible all of their lives find they can gain insight almost every time they open its pages. Changing the ways they read and study Scripture helps them discover fresh perspectives from time to time. To get the most from your reading, try some of these approaches:

- Read actively by highlighting meaningful phrases and jotting down your response in a journal or along the margins.
- Read devotionally by meditating on the words of a short passage and asking the Holy Spirit to speak to you through the words you are reading.
- Use Bible dictionaries and commentaries to learn about the historical background, original languages, and meanings of difficult passages. You can also use a concordance to find what the Bible has to say about a topic that interests you.
- Read a passage in several different translations (using a parallel Bible or a website like BibleGateway.com).
- Join a Bible study or simply read along with another Christian to share insight, encouragement, and help.

*They [who] delight in the law of the LORD . . . prosper in all they do.*   PSALM 1:2-3